FRIDAY'S CHILD

Books by Michele Poague

Fiction
Heir to Power – 2010
Fall of Eden – 2011
Ransom – 2015
The Candy Store – 2015
The Broken Shade – 2020

Nonfiction
Friday's Child – 2023

Nonfiction co-authored by
Debbie Matthews and Michele Poague
Riding Shotgun – 2020

FRIDAY'S CHILD

By Michele Poague

*I believe in God, not because my parents told me,
not because the church told me, but because I have
experienced His grace and mercy myself.*

Bent Briar Publishing LLC
Lakewood, Colorado 80223

Friday's Child ©2023 by Michele Poague.

Friday's Child is autobiographical. Names, places, businesses, organizations, events, and incidents are accurate to the best of the author's knowledge. Last names were intentionally not included.

Cover design by Michele Poague
Interior design by Michele Poague & Lois Deveneau

 Bent Briar Publishing LLLP
Lakewood, CO 20226
roseliterary@aol.com

ISBNS
978-1-942665-19-9 SC
978-1-942665-20-5 EPUB

First Edition: April 2023

10 9 8 7 6 5 4 3 2 1

This book is dedicated to every child of God who has ever felt lost and alone. Know that you are loved.

ACKNOWLEDGMENTS

I thank my editors, Ed Hinspeter, Kristen Coupal, Bette Rose Ryan, and Lois Deveneau, who stood by me and helped me complete this work. I thank the Calvary Chapel Cherry Creek members for their guidance and love. Through the teachings of pastors Matt Kornitotes and Jon Coupal, I came to understand the Bible and how God's grace has saved my life.

I give special thanks to Lois Deveneau, my friend and confidant. I could only have completed my previous seven books with her outstanding design and formatting skills.

This work was inspired by several books, including, *A Purpose Driven Life* by Rick Warren, *Jesus Calling* by Sarah Young, *The Indwelling Life of Christ* by Major W. Ian Thomas, and *In the Company of Jesus* by Bill Donahue. Of course, the Holy Bible, in its many translations, gave me tremendous inspiration and guidance throughout these months of writing.

Monday's child is fair of face.

Tuesday's child is full of grace.

Wednesday's child is full of woe.

Thursday's child has far to go.

Friday's child is loving and giving.

Saturday's child will work for a living.

But the child born on the Sabbath day

Is bonny and bright and good and gay.

Preface

This is the story of God's work in my life. His angels watched over and protected me from the day I was born. Long before I chose to be baptized, He laid out my path, knowing I would see the light many years and many heartbreaks later. As we grow older, our past begins to make sense, and patterns emerge. What I couldn't understand at twenty years old became clear at sixty. Looking at my past through the Word of God gives meaning and insight into my life's trials.

I believe hyper-independence is the result of trauma. "I don't need anybody and must do everything myself" actually means, "My ability to trust has been injured by people letting me down, failing me, or hurting me." We are born with the desire to control our lives and everything in it. Being out of control is scary if you don't have someone you can trust. Trusting God is the overreaching theme of the Bible.

Before this writing, I was a very different person. This is a story of redemption, but much like the Bible, it includes incest, rape, drugs, adultery, suicide, and subjects unsuitable for young people. For those people mentioned in this book, or those who know them, please understand it is not my intention to "out" any secrets, point fingers, or lay blame. I have sinned as much, if not more, than any of the people I mention here. I will only brush on many anecdotes, leaving others to share the details of their stories if they wish.

In this manuscript, I face the darkest parts of my soul and share my sins in the hope that you will see what the Lord has done in my life. You cannot know the true power of God's Grace unless you understand the great lengths the devil will go to destroy you. I'm only able to understand this after my salvation in 2021. Please do not pity me for anything I may have endured. It is because of sin that I have found the Lord Jesus Christ.

Proverbs 30
2 I am more stupid than any other person, and I lack a human's ability to understand. 3 I have not gained wisdom, and I have no knowledge of the Holy One.
[CSB]

Foundation

Psalm 139
13For it was you who created my inward parts; you knit
me together in my mother's womb. **14** I will praise you
because I have been remarkably and wondrously made.
Your works are wondrous, and I know this very well.
15 My bones were not hidden from you when I was made
in secret, when I was formed in the depths of the earth.
16 Your eyes saw me when I was formless; all my days
were written in your book and planned before a single
one of them began.
[CSB]

I was born in December of 1956. My parents lived in Denver, Colorado, at the time, but they were home for the holidays, so I was born in the little town of Newman Grove, Nebraska. I'm the middle, of the middle child of a family of six girls and one boy, each born on a different day of the week.

I am Friday's Child.

1953 – Bette Rose – Thursday
1954 – Robert Lee – Saturday
1955 – Belinda May – Wednesday
1956 – Michele Rae – Friday
1958 – Debra Kay – Sunday
1959 – Christine Dee – Tuesday
1969 – Mari Joleen – Monday

☙📖❧

My first memory, about the age of three, was moving into the house on 1st Avenue during the summer of 1959. Debbie was a baby, and my mom was eight months pregnant with Christine. I was sitting on our new front step while my mom carried Debbie and boxes from our rust-colored station wagon into the house. I was a loner and rarely played with my older siblings. My mom called me Mousy because I was so quiet. My immediate family calls me Micky.

My mom had her hands full with six children in seven years. It seems fitting that my only brother was born on Saturday, and Debra, born three months premature with Cerebral Palsy, was born on the Christian Sabbath of Sunday.

Growing up with a disabled sibling gives one a different worldview. For us, visiting Children's Hospital for physical therapy twice a week was routine. We never thought twice about having braces, crutches, and a wheelchair around the house. The boy across the street also had Cerebral Palsy, and he was our good friend. Dressing Debbie in her heavy braces each morning was hard work and a duty I didn't like, but looking back on it now, I see it was a gift.

James 1
2 Dear brothers and sisters, when troubles of any kind come your way, consider it an opportunity for great joy. 3 For you know that when your faith is tested, your endurance has a chance to grow.
[NLT]

࿆📖࿆

I don't remember a time my mom didn't work, and my father was rarely home. He worked two jobs and had a lot of hobbies, like bowling and skiing. When he was home, my father often napped on the couch while taping country songs on his reel-to-reel tape recorder.

With my mom working Sundays, we rarely had the opportunity to attend church. Occasionally church members would pick us up and bring us home again. When the weather was nice, we would sometimes walk. Grace Baptist was about a mile from our home. When Debbie wore her braces, she could make the long walk until she had surgery on her tendons. Unfortunately, once she was in a wheelchair, it was too difficult to push her up the hills. Because of our sporadic attendance, I never bonded with the church. Of course, I heard the stories about Jesus, Mary and Joseph, and David and Goliath. The Sunday School stories didn't have any meaning beyond stories about people who lived long ago.

&~📖~&

On one of these Sunday afternoons, I remember my father touching me in a way that made me afraid to be with him. I was four or possibly five. I don't know where my other siblings were right then. I can only remember trying to get away. I thank God that the full impact of that event didn't hit me until I was nearly forty. I believe God protects children from things their minds are too young to handle by disconnecting our emotions from our thoughts. Sometimes, He erases the memory entirely.

One day when I was seven, my father was leaving for the bowling alley, and when he kissed me goodbye, he stuck his tongue in my mouth. I thought it was gross, and it made me uncomfortable. The invasive effect of that inappropriate kiss didn't hit me until I was fifteen.

I don't know enough about psychology to understand why we do what we do or crave the things we crave. I don't know if nature or nurture causes a child to be curious about sex at an incredibly young age. I was wonton, promiscuous, and curious long before I was old enough to understand my body. At age five, I began experimenting with my brother and cousins. I did shameful things just to be liked. I confused lust with love. This affliction would rule my life for over fifty years. Trust me when I say you cannot judge me any harsher than I judge myself.

❧ 📖 ❧

My mom worked at the bakery and paid half the house and utility payments. One would think we would have had a lot of nice things with two working parents in the early 1960s, but my father's hobbies were expensive. We had a color TV, a speed boat, a camper, and a new truck, but only one pair of shoes each. We weren't exactly poor. Although we couldn't afford milk other than what was for our cereal in the morning.

The boat, camper, and truck belonged to my father. In his defense, he worked hard and didn't want to spend his money on things like school clothing. He grew up with one set of work clothes and one set of school clothes, so that should be good enough for his kids. We got a new outfit every Easter and a new pair of shoes yearly. The girls shared toys, beds, and clothing.

I remember one evening, the only thing in the house to make for dinner was a can of lima beans. My mom was at work, and my father made dinner. He bribed us to eat by offering a dime to whoever finished first and a nickel for second place. I believe Debbie and Belinda got a dime, while Robert and Bette got a nickel. Christine and I never did eat the beans, so we obviously weren't starving.

I hated school because I was bullied by the neighbor boys in first and second grade. They would throw rocks at me and call me Icky Micky. I'm sure it was because I was timid. The taunting left scars on my psyche. I believed I was ugly and stupid until well after high school. In the third grade, I had my first real friend, Diana. Bullies run in groups, and if you have a friend, they tend to find another loner.

❧📖❧

From 1962 through 1966, there was a lot of fighting between my parents. My older siblings fought as well. These fights were often quite violent. I watched my brother push my sister down the stairs one day. I came home from a friend's house, and my brother was lying on the floor, covered in bloody scratches from my sisters. I usually found a closet to hide in until the fight was over. To this day, I hate hearing people argue, but that's not to say I don't have a temper of my own.

In 1966, my parents had a terrible fight, and my father moved out. I didn't know the reasons until I was much older. I respect my mom for what she went through. Raising six children as a single parent couldn't have been easy. Divorce wasn't common; it was something that happened to movie stars and bad people. I was ashamed to tell anyone. During the first few months of their separation, my father lived in his camper behind the gas station, where he worked part-time.

That year I had trouble concentrating at school. If a child can be depressed, that is the best description of what I was going through. I spent all my time daydreaming and not paying attention to the teachers. I suffered from stomach cramps that continued for several years. I was even more withdrawn.

When I did play with Christine or Robert, my favorite game was "Runaways." I would make up an elaborate story about not having parents and living in an abandoned car or train. The game was all about figuring out how to get food and keep warm. We pretended the abandoned car was in a ditch behind a grocery store, and we could sneak an extension cord from the store to the car. We pretended to shoplift our food. I don't know if my brother and sister felt the same sense of control over their lives by playing this game as I did.

Our lifestyle didn't change much with the divorce, but I have no idea how hard it was for my mom. Debbie needed to go to Physical Therapy twice a week. She had to shop, do laundry, and clean the house, all while holding down a full-time job. She worked Sundays and holidays because the bread had to be in the stores on Mondays and the day after a holiday. She worked all the overtime she could get because it paid more. She was a solid example of personal responsibility.

About this time, our church sent over some children's clothing. My mom was so embarrassed and angry. She yelled at my older sister for telling the church we would take the donation. She said she didn't need the church to supply clothes for her children. She was proud and independent.

❧📖❧

I spent the summer of 1967 on my grandparents' farm in Nebraska. It was enjoyable because I was alone with my thoughts most of the time. Children have very vivid imaginations, and I have always been good at entertaining myself.

The farm taught me to be responsible. I had several daily chores, like gathering eggs, feeding the hogs, and walking to the end of the driveway to pick up the mail. One day, a letter came addressed to my brother, who was also working on the farm that summer, and me. My grandmother saw that the return address was from Mr. & Mrs. Robert Jeffryes.

She said, "It's from your mom," and began to read, "Your dad and I were married last week at a little church…." Without waiting any longer, I ran out to the field to tell my brother that mom and dad got remarried.

We were so happy as we came running back to the house. I think most children hope their parents will reunite one day. When we returned, my grandmother clarified that the letter was from Patricia, my father's girlfriend, not our mom. I had never been so crushed. I cried all day and well into the night.

On the farm, we went to church every Sunday, but my biblical education was limited to a couple of summers. I knew a few bible stories, and if someone asked me if I was a Christian, I would say I was Baptist but didn't understand the meaning of God's Word or salvation.

Later that year, my sister and brother were fighting about chores. When my mom came out to see what was happening, Robert grabbed a shovel and threatened her. He had a temper much like our father. He was as large as my mom when he was in the eighth grade, so he went to live with my father and stepmother. I think this was good for him, but what proved to be better was the many summers he attended church regularly. I don't know when he was baptized, but I know he had many friends from church.

I was in the fifth grade when I met Vicky. She was very precocious. Within months, she had me ending my friendship with Diana. She dominated my life for the next two years. She taught me how to steal, how to smoke cigarettes, how to skip classes, and how to sew. She had access to adult clothing, and we would dress up like "teenagers." At eleven, I was far from looking like a teenager, but the idea was to get boys to look at us. We would walk down busy streets, hoping someone would honk or whistle.

Freddy lived two houses away, and he was adorable. He was in eighth grade, and I was in the sixth. That seemed like a vast age difference at the time. He always whistled or said something about how cute we were, so I walked past his house every chance I got. I hate to admit it, but I liked the attention. I also liked the idea of being grown up. It was another form of the runaway game.

Debbie had her Physical Therapy on Tuesdays and Thursdays. Working nights allowed my mom to shop for groceries and take us to the doctor or dentist without missing work. Bette was fourteen and old enough to babysit her younger siblings at night. Sometimes, after my mom left for work, Bette and Belinda snuck out of the house to meet older boys. That left me to watch Debbie and Christine. I was eleven, and we were already in bed, so it wasn't a burden. I don't know if I didn't tell my mom because I wanted my sisters to like me or if I just didn't care where they went.

Saturday was our day with my father. He usually took us to the bowling alley. It was the only regular time we had with him. I never felt like he wanted to spend time with us because he worked the entire day.

He signed Bette, Robert, Belinda, and me up for junior league bowling. I was the youngest on the team. I was terrible and absolutely hated always coming in last. I would have preferred playing in the nursery with Christine and Debbie. To this day, I've never joined a league of any kind. I don't have a competitive instinct. After bowling, we would have dinner with him and my stepmother and come home.

The following summer, Robert turned fourteen, and Belinda was almost thirteen. The three of us went to Nebraska for the summer. Christine was too young to do chores, and

Debbie was disabled, so they stayed in Denver with Bette. Robert stayed with my father's parents near Genoa, and Belinda and I stayed with my mom's parents outside Albion, Nebraska.

One night, Belinda confided in me that she was going to have a baby. Our maternal grandparents were highly religious, and she was afraid to tell them. I felt terrible for her.

The remainder of this story is for her to share, but the event caused quite a stir in the family. I wish I had been old enough to give her the support she sorely needed. At eleven, I barely understood how a pregnancy occurred. Shortly after, she was also sent to live with my father.

❧📖❧

My stepmother, Pat, made good money, so they lived in a nicer house in a good-quality neighborhood. Belinda and Robert each had a room of their own and lots of new clothes. I still shared a room with Christine. Belinda tried to give me some clothes she no longer wanted, and instead of being thankful, I felt she was mocking me for being poor. It was five years before I recognized that I had been envious and another ten years before I understood her life was much more complicated than I had realized.

Early in 1969, Belinda and Robert attended Applewood Baptist Church in Lakewood. They invited me to join them, and after a few visits, I found myself at the front of the church, asking Jesus to come into my life. I was confused and hurting in ways I can't describe. The draw of Jesus Christ was strong, and the offer of peace was seductive. I honestly felt changed after my baptism. I promised God I would be a better person. Unfortunately, when I got home from my baptism, my parents were still divorced, and my mom had recently married a man I didn't respect. I tried not to be angry with family members, but I wasn't strong enough. My older sister was left in charge while my mom worked and Vern was on the road. Based on the summers of her sneaking out of the house, I had little respect for her.

We had few material things compared to my father's family, so I was envious. My raging hormones were wreaking havoc on my body. I had always been sickly thin, looking more like a twig than a girl. During that summer, I went from having a perfect 36" figure of (12" -12" -12") to a perfect 36" figure of 36" -26" -34". Worst of all, I still battled with my out-of-control lust and an anger I couldn't quiet.

Vicky moved away, and I rekindled my friendship with Diana.

Matthew 4
*¹"Then Jesus (after his baptism) was led by the Spirit
into the wilderness to be tempted by the devil. ²After
fasting forty days and forty nights, He was hungry. ³The
tempter came to him and said, "If you are the Son of
God, tell these stones to become bread." ⁴Jesus answered,
"It is written: 'Man shall not live on bread alone, but on
every word that comes from the mouth of God."⁵Then
the devil took him to the holy city and had him stand on
the highest point of the temple. ⁶"If you are the Son of
God," he said, "throw yourself down. For it is written:
"He will command his angels concerning you, and they
will lift you up in their hands, so that you will not strike
your foot against a stone."'Jesus answered him (the
devil), "It is also written: 'Do not put the LORD your
God to the test.'"*
[NIV]

I needed Christ but didn't know how to ask
for help. Applewood Baptist Church was across
town, and I didn't like Grace Baptist, so my
attendance was sketchy.

They tell me that when you turn to Christ,
the devil attacks. I can see it now, years later. I
spiraled downward into depression over the next
several years. I started drinking, ran away from
home, and put myself in more than a few life-
threatening situations.

Tribulation

Jeremiah 29

11 "For I know the plans I have for you," declares the LORD, "plans to prosper you and not to harm you, plans to give you hope and a future. 12 Then you will call on me and come and pray to me, and I will listen to you. 13 You will seek me and find me when you seek me with all your heart.
[NLT]

I t has always been a part of my personality to run away from anything I find unpleasant. I was a loner, more comfortable in my own company than with my siblings. I had a vivid imagination and could entertain myself for hours.

During the summer of 1969, I ran away from home for a couple of weeks. Taking care of myself wasn't as easy as the game I played. At thirteen, I could get food from friends and a place to stay, but it came at a cost. One of the young men expected sex in exchange for a place to sleep. I wasn't a stranger to intercourse, as I'd experimented with a boy who lived a couple of blocks from our house the previous year. I was uncomfortable trading my body for a place to stay, so I returned home. I would run away from home again at ages fifteen, sixteen, and seventeen. I didn't realize then, though it is so clear now that I was trying to run away from myself and my demons.

As time passed, I got to know Freddy, the boy who lived two houses away. He would often call me over to his front porch, where we would sit and talk for hours. One winter day in 1969, he invited me into his house. We sat on the couch talking. After a while, he kissed me.

When he put his tongue in my mouth, I totally freaked out. I remembered my father sticking his tongue in my mouth. I burst into tears and started shaking. I couldn't tell Freddy why I

[18]

had run away that day. I'm sure he thought he'd done something terribly wrong. I was already angry with my father for leaving us and marrying another woman. Now I was mad at him for ruining what might have been a beautiful first kiss.

◈📖◈

Janice, a girl of twenty-one, lived across the street from Diana. During the Summer of 1970, she invited us to an adult party with alcohol and adult men in attendance. I drank Sloe Gin and Squirt because I didn't like the taste of beer or whiskey.

This was my first time being intoxicated. It made me feel grown-up, happy, and sexy. As an introverted teen, alcohol gave me the courage to talk to strangers and dance like no one was watching. I flirted with the men.

A friend of Janice's offered to get more alcohol and asked me to ride along. Instead of going to the liquor store, Mike drove outside the city to a well-known make-out place. I had been flirting and didn't think much about kissing him in the car.

Mike was twice my size, and soon he began forcing himself on me. I didn't want to have sex, but I felt guilty for flirting with him. I felt helpless. I cried and begged him to stop, but he didn't. I couldn't tell anyone because I was underage and drunk. My mom would kill me if she found out what I had done.

As I said earlier, I was curious and experimented with sex. I was precocious. I learned to masturbate by age six. While I was lustful, I always wanted to be the one to decide where and when. Unfortunately, men are usually more robust and in control. This wouldn't be the last time I found myself in harm's way.

A few days later, I found a book in the library on black magic. I cast a spell, hoping he would die for what he had done to me. The next day, Bette told me Mike had died in the hospital. I'm unsure if she was telling the truth or trying to scare me. Although I never learned the truth, I never touched black magic again. I was never good when faced with temptation, and I would test God's love for me in almost every way imaginable over the next fifty years.

When I realized how broken and sin-filled I was, I tried to blot out the light of the Holy Spirit.

~📖~

In the early autumn of 1971, I was fourteen years old. Alone in my room at two in the morning, I had a bottle of barbiturates in my hand as I asked God to understand why I was about to take my life. I prayed in desperation. I recall a long conversation with God. Because God knows everything, I knew He would understand my pain.

I was hurting in a way I cannot describe even to this day. My emotions and hormones were out of control, causing rage and fear to wrack my body daily. I felt possessed. It was so painful that I simply didn't believe I could go on. I felt like I was drowning.

As most people do before taking their life, I tried to put things in order. I cleaned my room and then wrote a note to my family. It was angry and hurtful because I was angry and hurting. Once done, I got on my knees and asked God to let me go, knowing he could see my pain and would understand. This would mark the first time I earnestly prayed for anything.

At about four in the morning, I took my sister's seizure medication and went to bed. It was my turn to dress Debbie for her school bus, so I was supposed to be up by six. When I didn't get up, my older sister started hitting me with a belt thinking I was being stubborn. I couldn't move. I didn't feel the belt, but my hearing was fine. Bette called the hospital, but she thought I'd taken the pills around one. When my mom got home from work, my sister's husband (Bette was recently married at seventeen) told my mom I was faking and would be fine. Then I stopped breathing, followed by a trip to the hospital.

When I woke up in the emergency room, I was angrier than I had ever thought possible. It's hard to describe how defeated you can feel when you fail to take your own life. It was only one more thing I couldn't do right. I was angry at myself for not taking the pills before I cleaned my room. I was angry with my family for not letting me go. I thought, if there is a God, He wasn't listening to me. I didn't blame God; I dismissed Him, believing that if He truly loved me, He would have let me go and ended my pain.

Many things led me to this point of desperation, including the rape and fear of my own rage. The will to survive is the strongest of all our instincts. This is not a popular belief, but I think if someone is in so much pain that they are willing to take their life, it is selfish of us to ask them to keep going. Yes, it is a permanent solution to a temporary problem, and if you can help someone find the light in their darkest hour, please do. Cursing them will not alleviate your pain or anyone else's pain. Their life belongs to God. He won't take them if he isn't ready for them. Apparently, God wasn't finished with me.

Although I would think about killing myself thousands of times after this, I never went further than driving to a cliff's edge. I would like to say the pain eased over the next few years, but sadly, that wasn't the case.

When the Lord has saved you, the devil can't destroy you, so he does everything in his power to distract you.

Matthew 26
11 Watch and pray that you may not enter into
temptation. The spirit indeed is willing, but the flesh is
weak."
(ESV)

After my attempted suicide, my mom moved our family to Sioux Falls, South Dakota, in October of 1971.

Belinda came to live with us in January 1972. I didn't know the details, but it seemed she had a falling out with my father and stepmother. Belinda and I were closer now. I was starting to understand how hard her life had been in those last years that we lived in Denver. I was still envious of her. She was beautiful and intelligent and seemed to have her life together.

We were living in Norton Acres on the north side of Sioux Falls. It was a small subdivision of about sixteen square blocks. Interestingly, there were more than twenty kids ages twelve to eighteen in that small neighborhood. For the first time, I had friends and was rather popular.

Unfortunately, my new popularity didn't make me any smarter.

My friend, Jeannie, turned sixteen about nine months before me. Her parents gave her a Ford Pinto for her birthday. You can get into a bundle of trouble when you have the freedom a car provides. Jeannie knew a family where the parents were usually away playing bingo or drinking at the bar. Their eight kids, ages ten to seventeen, had access to marijuana and alcohol. I didn't dare to try marijuana, but I liked how alcohol made me feel.

I had a crush on a boy of thirteen. In my drunkenness, I tried to entice him to have sex with me. He was shy and probably too young. When he left the room, his older brother came in and forced me to give him what I had offered his brother. Even though I was drunk, I tried to fight him off. I screamed for several minutes, but no one came to my rescue. When it was over, I was angry, but part of me felt like I had it coming for how I had treated Donny.

Humans, dominated by their flesh, silence God's voice and resist the Holy Spirit's claims. As I mentioned earlier, I wasn't a stranger to my sexuality. Lust would be my reigning demon for many years.

∽📖∾

During the summer of 1972, my friend Diana came to visit from Denver. After about a week, I decided I wanted to return to Denver with her. Diana and I tried to hitchhike from Sioux Falls to Denver. We got as far as Sioux City, Iowa, before being arrested by the police. I spent two days in jail before I told them who I was. My mom came to get me and dropped me off on the farm in Nebraska for the rest of the summer, hoping I wouldn't get into more trouble. I didn't mind being alone on the farm, but I missed having access to cigarettes.

At the end of the summer, I went back to South Dakota and attended most of my sophomore year at Washington High School. I was still having problems with stomach pain, and my menses were anything but regular. I was given antibiotics for a low-grade infection. The infection would get better for a few weeks and then return with a vengeance. I tried to ignore the pain, but I started missing school regularly.

During this winter, 1972 to 1973, I met my first husband, Jeff. He was eighteen but naive about sex. I taught him everything I'd learned, which was far more than a sixteen-year-old girl should know.

Belinda graduated in January of 1973 and moved back to Colorado to live with her boyfriend, Jimmy. Again, I was jealous of her freedom.

One would think I should have learned after the first two times I ran away that it really isn't a good idea.

When spring came, I dropped out of school and ran away again. This time, I took the bus. While in Denver, I stayed with Belinda and Jimmy and worked at Burger King. About two months into the living arrangements, Belinda and I started fighting about money. Belinda was using my rent money to help pay for her wedding. At sixteen, I probably didn't understand finances well, but the bur under my saddle had more to do with her choice of a husband than my need to keep more of my income. I didn't have the heart to tell her that her boyfriend had tried to sexually assault me while she was at work. Though I was not a virgin, I was particular with whom I was willing to share my body, and my sister's boyfriends were off-limits.

I moved in with Diana and her parents to avoid Jimmy and Belinda. When my mom and family came to Denver for Belinda's wedding in June, they took me back to South Dakota. I was willing to go because I had severe stomach pains with no doctor or money for medicine. A week later, I had an appendectomy.

After my surgery, Jeff and I rekindled our relationship. Through him, I met his brother, Bill, and his girlfriend, Marian. Bill was twenty-four, and Marian was twenty-two. They rented a small apartment on Tenth Street in Sioux Falls. Over the next four years, Marian and I became close friends.

In August of 1973, we moved to Valley Springs, a town of fewer than five hundred people. It felt like my friends had been ripped away again. At least this time, it was only sixteen miles, not six hundred.

I attended Brandon Valley High during my Junior year of high school. After the appendicitis surgery, I still had significant problems with my reproductive system. I was on half a dozen different medications and missed more school than I attended.

I still managed to hitchhike into Sioux Falls regularly to meet with Jeff or Bill and Marian. One time I started walking the sixteen miles into town at two in the morning. The temperature was minus ten. On the highway, about a mile out of town, a guy I knew from playing pool at the bar was coming back from Sioux Falls. He offered to give me a ride to Bill and Marian's apartment. When I look back, I am amazed at my sheer stupidity. The only answer I can think of is that God was watching over me. He had a plan for me all along.

By this age, I could pass for twenty-one and often went to bars with Bill and Marian. When we weren't at the bars, we smoked a lot of pot. We tried LSD, and they introduced me to speed.

Jeff and I had a very on-and-off relationship. Jeff liked a girl named Marie and couldn't decide which of us he wanted. I befriended Marie and sometimes stayed with her when I was in town.

The J&M Club was a rough bar, but they had some great local bands. I went with Bill and Marian on my seventeenth birthday to see the band Starchild. While there, Bill asked his friend to give me a ride back to their apartment so I could show him the way.

I don't remember the man's name, but he said he had to stop at his place to pick something up. He led me past four men watching TV in the living room and into his bedroom. He pulled out a knife and told me that if I didn't have sex with him, he would call the men in the other room, who would hold me down and take turns. He may have been bluffing, but I didn't take the chance. I didn't know any of those men, and my history with men wasn't exactly stellar.

When he finally dropped me off at Bill and Marian's place (he didn't come in), I yelled at Bill for setting me up with this jerk of a man and walked out. It was December in South Dakota, and four in the morning. Luckily, I was only ten blocks from Marie's apartment, and my anger kept me warm. As mad as I was at Bill, I didn't understand why I seemed to be a magnet for rapists.

&📖&

Jeff's older sister, Debbie, had a small house by Covell Park. I dropped out of school and moved in with her in April of 1974. Foolishly, I didn't have the money or way to continue my various medications. By June, I was extremely sick. I was so weak from blood loss I couldn't sit up without someone holding me. Jeff carried me to the car and took me to my doctor, who immediately sent me to the Emergency Room. I was nearly unconscious by the time we arrived at the hospital. Because my blood pressure was dangerously low, the hospital gave me an immediate blood transfusion.

During an exploratory surgery to see what was going on in my reproductive system, they removed my left Fallopian tube and part of my uterus. The doctor described my female organs as "ground hamburger" from massive infection. Sadly, because I was only seventeen, they didn't take everything while they were in there. Although I had less than a one percent chance of getting pregnant, they left as much as possible. Ten years later, I would have a total hysterectomy, including ovaries and the right fallopian tube.

My mom took me in once more during my recovery, but she made it clear I wasn't to stay once I was on my feet again. I was a bad influence on my younger sisters. Two months later, I moved in with Marie.

I was just beginning to understand how much my mother loved me, like trying to understand God's love for us. I was defiant, angry, and hurtful, yet she was always there for me when I needed her. I ran away from God after my baptism, but like my mom, He was always there, looking after me, whispering in my ear, and loving me, though I fought him at every turn. God was there for me even if I refused to see it. *Mom, forgive me for the pain I put you through, and thank you for never giving up on me.* "Lord, forgive me for the pain I put you through and thank you for never giving up on me. Amen."

Psalm 8
⁴ *what is mankind that you are mindful of them, human beings that you care for them?*
(NIV)

∂📖∽

Jeff and I got married in July of 1975. I didn't understand marriage or commitment. We fought over money and my pride. Jeff wasn't working steadily and was willing to take handouts from his parents. I was far too proud. He was not ambitious, being content to have little or nothing if it left him time to play with his cars or go fishing. I was tired of being poor, wanted nice things, and worked hard at any job I could land. We split up in January of 1976 when I went to work at the Macamba Club. We got back together in June and then split the following December.

Back in 1974, Jimmy had joined the army. Shortly after, he and Belinda moved to Germany, where my nephew was born. When they returned to the States in 1976, they moved to Valley Springs, South Dakota, just down the street from my mom. I'd seen them on a few occasions over the next year. I was separated from Jeff and wasn't close to my sister. I knew Jimmy was given a dishonorable discharge from the service, but I didn't have many details. The following year, after Belinda and Jimmy divorced, Belinda moved in with me for a couple of months. I was too wound up in my own problems to see how much she needed my help.

❧📖❧

Discotheques were all the rage in 1977. I was twenty when I started working at the Disconnection nightclub. I sold tickets at the front door at night and cleaned the club during the day for extra money. I'd moved into a new one-bedroom apartment I couldn't afford. Without a car, I had to hitchhike to work and hoped someone would give me a ride home at night. I was living on carrots and celery because it was the only thing I could afford.

One mid-August night, Jimmy came into the club. I was nice to him and filled him in on what was happening in my life. Belinda had recently moved to Montana with her new husband, so I was surprised Jimmy was still in Sioux Falls.

The next morning, Jimmy showed up at my house. Never giving it a thought, I let him in. He'd been drinking and was saying off-color things. I tried to get him to leave. My friend, Brad, was scheduled to pick me up in about an hour to clean the nightclub.

When Jimmy attacked me, I didn't back down. I couldn't understand why this was happening to me again. I was angry and fighting, but he was much stronger than me. Although I did my best to get away, he straddled me, and his hands closed around my throat. I could see his knife not five inches from my hand, but I couldn't use it. It had been eight years since I had reached out to God. I was in a situation so far out of my control that it was the only place I could turn. Jimmy was squeezing the life from me. As I began to lose conciseness, I prayed. I prayed to a God I claimed I didn't believe in. I prayed for the first time since my attempted suicide. That morning I begged Him to help me. "God," I prayed, "please don't let me die like this."

I had refused to acknowledge God for years, but when I was in real trouble, I begged for His help.

Psalm 138
3 In the day when I cried out, You answered me, And made me bold with strength in my soul.
(NKJV)

God answered, and I lived. Once more, He wasn't ready for me. When I came to, seconds later, the fight in me had died. When Jimmy was done, he let me up, and I ran to the bathroom. While I was changing out of my torn clothes, Brad came to take me to work. Jimmy let him in the door and left. Finding myself in that position again was humiliating. I was too ashamed to tell Brad what had happened, too distraught to go to work that afternoon. Brad let me stay at his house and went on to the club. By evening, I had pulled myself together enough to go to work.

I was fine until Jimmy called the club asking if I had told anyone what had happened. I completely fell apart. I sat in the corner of the ticket booth, crying and shaking. My boss saw me panic-stricken and trembling and took me back to his office. The club had an off-duty cop working the door, and Brad told Bob something had been wrong with me since he had picked me up that morning.

Bob was more insistent in his questioning. I broke down and told them what had happened. After filing a police report outlining the details, Bob took me to the hospital. I was released after an intimidating and insensitive physical. Instead of going home, I went to Jeff's house. I couldn't bear to be alone.

I didn't know why my life was spared, and in my arrogance, I still thought I was in control. Although I was glad to have survived, I didn't repent or thank God for saving my life. I chalked my survival up to fate and my giving into Jimmy's demands.

There was an arrest warrant for Jimmy, but he left the state. I tried to put the incident out of my mind the best I could, hoping I would never see him again.

Romans 1
²¹ For though they knew God, they did not glorify him as God or show gratitude. Instead, their thinking became worthless, and their senseless hearts were darkened.
(CSB)

❧📖❦

Jeff made me quit my job at the nightclub. He wanted me at home or with him all the time. For a while, that was okay. I hated being around people. Without me working, we couldn't afford the apartment on north Spring Avenue, so we moved.

I hated the new apartment, but I was afraid to be alone. I felt like I was drowning. I became severely depressed. I just wanted to go to sleep and never wake up again, but suicide was too much work.

Jeff and I fought over money, but more than that, we fought over whom I wanted to be. I got my GED and applied for a college student loan. Jeff hated the idea of me going back to school.

I learned something important during the year of my recovery. While there were few outward signs of the trauma, I couldn't wear a scarf or necklace without panic and terror. Not wanting to be around people gave me lots of time to reflect. I found myself asking why these terrible things kept happening to me. (There were other incest abuses and violence I won't recount here.) I'm a very logical thinker. My world needed to make sense. I came to believe these horrible experiences were necessary. My purpose was to experience life in all its pain and glory. That others had different, but just as tragic experiences only confirmed my belief. The entity that was my soul, and the soul of others, needed to experience EVERYTHING.

I concluded that the only things that were real were thought and emotion. Thought and feelings aren't tangible. You can't see them, but like the wind, you can see and feel their effects. I believed everything in our physical world was a manifestation of those two elements, neither of which can be quantified.

I was secure in my new philosophy because it made the pain make sense. My explanation of the Big Bang was that the universe was formed when willpower brought thought and emotion together. The purpose of this universe was for this entity, who had this incredible willpower, to experience every possible feeling and have every possible thought.

How many ways are there to die? How many ways are there to fall in love? How many different heartbreaks can we humans experience in a lifetime? Since our thoughts and emotions are influenced by our upbringing and experiences, even the exact same death would be perceived differently by different people.

With this theory in my pocket, everything that had happened to me, good or bad, was only an experience for me to share with the universe, nothing more. With this conviction, I could forgive myself for being stupid enough to be compromised so many times. I believed these experiences were meant to happen to me for the greater good, for the experience.

2 Corinthians 4
18 We set our eyes not on what we see but on what we cannot see. What we see will last only a short time, but what we cannot see will last forever.
(NCV)

❧ 📖 ❦

Shortly after I turned twenty-one, Jeff and I moved again to an even cheaper house. It was so small that you couldn't shut the bathroom door if you were standing at the sink. The bed took up the entire floor of the bedroom. We had to stand on the bed to reach anything in the closet. The dresser was in the living room.

Over the winter, Jeff had taken up with a new girlfriend, but I was so depressed I didn't care. I went out with Bill and Marian some evenings and occasionally went home with other men. Jeff and I talked about separating, but we hadn't made any move toward splitting. I really didn't have the energy or any place to go. I started working at a truck stop a few miles from the house in May.

Without boring you with the details, there were four times I completely lost control of my temper and went insane. The first three times, I was accused of something I didn't do. Try as I might, I wasn't believed, which made me angry.

One June day, as I was leaving for work, Jeff told me his girlfriend wanted to come over and spend the night. The full impact of the request didn't hit me until I was at work. I held it together until I got home, but then I was outraged by his proposal. Did he expect me to sleep on the couch?

Jeff was so flippant about it that I lost my mind and chased him out of the house. He took off in the car. I wanted to kill him and his girlfriend.

My life could have ended there and then, but circumstances didn't allow me to destroy my life. When I realized I had no idea where to find them, I broke the television with the shotgun. I shattered every window, dish, and glass in the house and then sliced up our waterbed with a butcher knife.

My loss of control scared me, and I swore I would never let anyone make me that angry again.

I vowed that I would never care that much about anyone or anything. I've not lost my temper like that since, but it hasn't been an easy road.

The ensuing week I moved into a small apartment downtown. My student loan came through, so I paid pay rent for the entire year. I still needed a job for food and school supplies, so I started working the grave shift at the 7-11 three blocks from my new apartment.

I spent most nights in the bars and days trying to get to work or school on time while squeezing in homework. My relationship with Bill and Marian had waned, so I found new friends.

This is who I am. I've always run away the moment a situation became difficult or when it no longer met my selfish needs. Unfortunately, no matter how far I tried to run away, I always woke up with myself.

෨෴

In August of that summer, Jimmy was extradited to South Dakota. I was called in front of the Grand Jury to bring the case to court. Because of my new philosophy, I was no longer angry or afraid of Jimmy. In fact, I felt sorry for him because I knew he was broken. He had to deal with his own life experiences that led him to my door.

After the Grand Jury Hearing, the District Attorney told me Jimmy was willing to plead guilty to attempted rape for a lesser sentence.

Jimmy was facing twenty years in maximum security prison. I told the DA that Jimmy did rape me, but I didn't think prison was the answer. I asked that he be sent to a mental facility so that he might be healed. Jimmy was broken. What he needed was help. Jimmy pled guilty and was remanded to a state mental health facility.

I was able to forgive Jimmy because I was broken. I understood his brokenness and believed he needed to have these experiences. That didn't mean the rape never happened, or I was okay with the assault, but my philosophy allowed me to let go of the fear and anger. I didn't have to be held prisoner to the anguish and shame. While I was reluctant to tell anyone about the incident, I moved on with my life.

After forgiving Jimmy, I could pardon other transgressions against me, like my father and the previous men who had raped me. I believed these experiences were necessary; they were not good or bad. I had dismissed all religions. I had decided how the universe came to be and the purpose of my life. My life motto was:

"Whatever doesn't kill you makes you stronger."

I was confident that through these trials, I would become greater than I was. I would grow stronger and develop empathy for others.

I had never read the Bible, so I didn't know about God's forgiveness. All of you Christians out there are nodding your head in understanding. You are fully aware of the power of forgiveness. I didn't know about the Bible's view on being grateful for the trials in our lives. I had never heard the stories of the Apostle Paul or Job. I only understood the story of Jesus in the broadest terms.

Writing this book many years later, I realize that The Holy Spirit had been whispering in my ear and guiding my thoughts and actions throughout my life. God truly works in mysterious ways.

❧📖☙

During the autumn of 1978, I attended Nettleton Business College because I had a crush on a guy attending school there. Sex has always been my strongest motivator. I should have dedicated myself to school, but at this little bar called Fritz's, I met a man named Bart who made me feel like a princess. I fell head over heels for him.

I dropped out of college the following March and moved to Las Vegas with Bart. I was still as wild as I had ever been, and Bart could match me when it came to the party. Although we cheated on each other a few times before moving to Nevada, we managed to stay together for four years. I never married Bart because I hadn't divorced Jeff.

In Las Vegas, I added crystal meth and gambling to my list of vices. I still had no control of my lustful demon and did terrible things, some Bart never discovered. I was drinking and staying at the casinos all night. Bart drank heavily and gambled as much as I did. He was mainly a danger to himself. Bart would stay out all night drinking or miss work because he was too drunk to go in. He often drove in this condition which made me crazy with worry.

It was in Las Vegas that I met Lois, my dearest friend. The friendship bond with her was stronger than any friend I had known. Like me, she had her own demons. We did foolish things together, but we were good for each other in the long run. We needed each other in those dark days.

❧ 📖 ❦

By 1982, I had spiraled into another deep depression and started dating a guitar player from a local band. I broke up with Bart and moved in with Jerry. I tried attending church several times but didn't know what questions to ask. That relationship lasted two years. Near the end of the relationship, I got sick again and had to have the remainder of my reproductive organs removed.

Drinking, gambling, and broken relation-ships had me on the run. I was a mess. I blew two thousand dollars one night at the Gold Strike

Casino in the autumn of 1984. I decided it was time to move back to Denver.

Bette had recently bought an old house in a rough part of town. There were holes in the walls, and stray cats had been living in the basement. Our plan was to remodel the house and sell it.

I needed a good-paying job to make the mortgage payments. My sister, Christine, suggested I work at a strip club near the store she managed. I was uncomfortable with the idea, but I applied at Shotgun Willie's when no other job materialized.

I called Lois, who was then living in North Carolina. I asked her to come to Denver and help me remodel the house. Decorating had been one of our deepest bonding issues in Nevada. She joined me in Colorado in the winter of 1984.

I worked as a cocktail waitress, the only work I had done since I was nineteen. I was shocked and embarrassed by the nudity, but the money was impressive.

Shortly after Lois and I moved into the house on Clarkson, the housing market tanked. Bette got married, and I was stuck in a barely livable place. I couldn't get a second mortgage because the home was appraised for less than we owed. I bought a dozen books on remodeling and ran up my credit cards, buying sheetrock, tools, and plumbing supplies.

To help pay for the remodeling work, Bette introduced me to a pleasant man who gave me money for sex. Sometimes he gave me cocaine. Wayne was sweet, and I liked spending time with him. When he started to talk about a more permanent relationship, I broke it off. I didn't know what I wanted to do with my life, but after Jeff, Bart, and Jerry, the thought of marriage terrified me.

While working at Shotgun Willie's, I was intimate with more men than I can recall. To say I was out of control would be putting it mildly. I was heavily involved with cocaine and drinking, which started affecting my job. I woke up one morning and realized that if I didn't make at least one hundred dollars that night, I wouldn't be able to make my house payment. That was my wake-up call. It would be another year before I reached rock bottom and two more years of constant struggle to break away from cocaine. I gave up my party friends, but I was still drinking too much and sleeping with way too many different men.

I had the occasional backslide with cocaine, but the episodes were further apart. While I didn't get on my knees and ask God to help me, I now know that somehow He was responsible for beating this demon. Like the night I took the barbiturates, I believe God had a plan for me.

In 1986 I discovered the Libertarian Party. I was drawn to their message of freedom coupled with responsibility. "Don't hurt people, and don't take their stuff." "Don't depend on the government to care for the poor because that is up to each of us." "You are free to do what you want, but you are not free from the consequences of your actions." The more I learned about Libertarian philosophy, the more involved I became. It was also a good distraction from drinking and drugs. Looking back, I believe I was led to the Libertarian Party to learn a whole new set of lessons.

By this time, Lois had met a wonderful man, married, and moved into their own place. We stayed close and tried a few business adventures. In 1985 Lois started working at The American Institute of Architects. When they had their annual convention in Colorado Springs, I volunteered to help. I had always dreamed of being an Interior Designer or Architect. I continued to volunteer for several years.

My father lived across town, so we spent the holidays with him. It was good to be near family. Although I had rationally forgiven him for the incidences when I was a child, I hadn't forgiven him emotionally. I wasn't prepared for him to touch me again inappropriately. I was saddened by his brokenness more than anything else. I wanted a relationship with him, but I could never trust him to be close enough to touch me. Like

Jimmy, I knew it was who he was, but I didn't have to be a part of it.

≈📖≪

Lois introduced me to Monte in 1988. He was a respectable and stable mailman. We began dating regularly, and my drug use and sexual exploits slowed down drastically. He worked from five in the morning until two in the afternoon. My schedule was eleven a.m. until seven at night. We usually got together on Monday night as I was off on Monday and Tuesday.

I didn't own a television, so I spent most Monday nights at his place watching Star Trek Next Generation. We liked the same books and movies. We both enjoyed camping, but while I liked warm beaches, he liked cool mountains.

Monte wanted to have children, something I couldn't give him, so we had an arrangement. Any time he met someone he thought could be the mother of his children, we would break up until he knew if the new relationship worked. We broke up about four times over the next ten years. Once, I broke up with him because I thought I'd met Mr. Right, someone who, for a brief moment, made me the center of his universe. As it turned out, he was looking for a mother.

While I had been clean for about a year, Charlie liked to smoke crack cocaine. My only rule about his use was never in my house. One day I came home from work to find him and a couple of friends smoking crack in my house. I kicked him out that night and never looked back.

When I turned thirty, I realized I needed a job I could still perform at sixty. Wearing a tiny uniform wouldn't be possible for much longer. I approached management with some ideas for better service and training. By this time, I had gotten over the shame of where I worked. I never told anyone where I worked for the first three years. As a trainer and hiring manager, I began to look at the business with a different eye. I wanted to make the job respectable. The term Gentlemen's Club meant a lot to me. I worked diligently to maintain the image of classy entertainment, a safe environment to work in, and a caring management staff. The responsibility kept me clean and mostly sober. Except for the occasional over-drinking, I had nearly pulled myself together.

I spent the next few years hiring and training waitresses at various clubs in several cities for International Entertainment Consultants. IEC was the company that managed Shotgun Willie's. The pay was terrible compared to what I made as a waitress, but I loved what I was doing.

When IEC terminated the contract with Shotgun Willie's in 1991, I started working for Lois at the American Institute of Architects.

The pay was even lower than IEC. I found myself faking receipts to skim money from petty cash to make ends meet. Being away from Shotgun Willie's meant I was away from the cocaine, and I could finally quit for good.

❧📖❦

My sisters and I were planning my father and stepmother's twenty-fifth-anniversary party during the summer of 1992. One morning I woke up from a horrifying nightmare. I couldn't stop crying. I was more frightened than I could ever remember. It was worse than that morning with Jimmy. The dream was about a monster under my bed which turned out to be my father. I was terrified. Although I could remember trying to get away from him when I was four, I had never attached any emotion to the incident; like it had happened to someone else. The full intensity of the event hit me through that nightmare.

Facing my father at his anniversary party a few days later was arduous. I believe the power of the Holy Spirit allowed me to be civil when all I wanted to do was run away screaming.

Nothing in the past had changed by reviving my emotional memories. I was still me, and my father was the same as he had always been. I

[47]

decided the universe sensed I was strong enough to handle trauma at thirty-five that would have broken me at five. I spent the next several months processing my feelings until I was able to set the anger and fear aside once more.

When I left the American Institute of Architects later that year, I went back to waitressing at Shotgun Willie's. Debbie Matthews was the majority owner who, along with George Miller, took an active role in the daily running of the business. In 1993 they asked me to be a floor manager. It was decent pay and steady hours. I had experience in scheduling, hiring, and training, but there was still a lot to learn about inventory and accounting.

One of Debbie's consultants, Dan Griffith, was a loving and generous man. He taught me the importance of caring about everyone who came through our doors. While I didn't have any real connection with the men who frequented the business, I really cared about the staff. I never equated my actions or feelings to Christ during those years, but I can see his influence now. I was never blind to the dark side of this business, and I did my best to protect the staff and inspire them to move on to better things.

Ephesians 4
15_Instead, we will speak the truth in love, growing in every way more and more like Christ, who is the head of his body, the church._
(NLT)

I believe the Holy Spirit uses you whenever he can, even if you aren't aware of it. I always disclosed the hard truth about the industry to prospective entertainers because I wanted them to make good decisions. Even though losing a new entertainer could hurt the business' bottom line. When a girl came to audition for the first time, I would tell her about the real dangers of the industry. I would stress how making lots of money could trap her in a lifestyle she couldn't keep up when her body gave out. In a few years, she would be tempted to do things she would later regret. I would tell her that many men would treat her badly and not respect her boundaries. Neighbors and family would disparage her. I warned her about drinking or taking drugs to make the job easier. My mission was to save every potential dancer from a life of debauchery.

I told myself that if she were going to dance for money, it would be better if she danced at Shotgun Willie's, where someone truly cared about her.

I never succeeded in talking anyone out of dancing; the lure of money was far too strong. I settled for trying to instill a sense of responsibility in all our employees. I urged them to have a plan when they grew older, so they wouldn't be tempted to do dangerous and more demeaning things to pay the bills. I encouraged them to attend college, save money for a house, or start a business. Sometimes, I would scold an employee, saying, "I don't want to see you still doing this in five years, and if you can't learn to be on time (or whatever), you won't qualify for anything else. Do you want to be a stripper forever?"

Drugs are prevalent in any service industry and are one of the most dangerous pitfalls of adult entertainment. Throughout the 80s and 90s, the company did regular drug screening tests to ensure none of the employees lost control. I was usually in charge of staff selection. About ten employees would be selected randomly. If the management team suspected an employee might be having problems with drugs, we made sure to test that employee as well. Our policy was that if employees tested positive for cocaine or opiates, they were required to bring back a clean UA in two days. If they could do that, it wasn't likely they had lost control. If they couldn't, we moved on to offer addiction rehabilitation at the company's expense. We included employees who had problems with alcohol. I'm still close to many employees who took advantage of our rehabilitation policies.

I never had my own children, but I felt a close connection to the women who passed through our doors. I remember times I almost quit my job because it hurt too much to lose an entertainer to drugs or the dark side of the adult entertainment business. I can't imagine what a parent feels like when a child goes astray and they can't pull them back. This gives me a new respect for how many times God gave his people another chance to be good. He must be aggrieved every time one of us stumbles over sin and idolatry.

Philippians 2
³Do nothing out of selfish ambition or conceit, but in humility consider others as more important than yourselves. ⁴Everyone should look not to his own interests, but rather to the interests of others.
(CSB)

As a manager, I was proud of the company. The owners of Shotgun Willie's were supportive and generous to their employees. When one of our bartenders was killed in a motorcycle accident, the owners opened a trust for his six-year-old daughter. They continued to pay the bartender's paycheck every week until she was eighteen. When a Disc Jockey died of a brain aneurysm, leaving behind a child, the club owners also opened a trust for her.

The owners also believed in giving back to the community. Every year the club would provide a "Feed the Homeless" dinner the week before Thanksgiving. All the employees chipped in to prepare and serve meals. We did a coat drive and gave every person who attended the dinner a blanket, socks, and gloves.

During the summer, the club organized a charity golf tournament, with the employees donating their day to the event. The proceeds went to any organization that wasn't too proud to take our money. Unfortunately, most large charities refused us, but some orphanages were willing to take the gift.

The entertainers often pitched in to help someone in need by raising money for them. An entertainer who had been paralyzed from a car accident needed a wheelchair. The club raised enough money to buy a brand-new motorized wheelchair. When an employee's sister lost three children and all her belongings in a house fire, the club raised several thousand dollars to replace the furnishings of someone they didn't even know.

When I wasn't working at the club, I was involved with the Libertarian Party. The first Presidential campaign I worked on was for Harry Browne in 1996 and again in 2000. Over the years, I served on several boards, including as State Chairman in 1998. I attended most of the National Conventions as a delegate and served as an Electoral College elector several times.

I enjoyed working outreach booths where I would introduce others to the philosophy and register them to vote. I helped collect signatures for several ballot initiatives and legislative bills.

Libertarian philosophy is about accepting your neighbor as they are. It's about not using the force of government to make others believe, do, or say what you believe, do, or say. The cornerstone sounds familiar to me now. Do the right thing, and don't judge others.

I stayed active in the Libertarian Party throughout the 1980s and 1990s. I served as State Chairman from 1998-1999 and co-produced the Libertarian State Conventions in 1998, 1999, 2000, and 2001. I continued to serve different positions on the State Board and to advise and assist in delivering several later state conventions.

I felt strongly that our country was in an economic meltdown, our public schools were failing, and we needed to return to a Restorative Justice System.

❧📖❧

Monte and I married in September of 1999. We were good friends, and Monte had given up on having his own children. While I was open to adoption, he was not. I wasn't comfortable with having a surrogate mother. I felt too many children needed good homes for us not to adopt when the time came to expand our family.

We bought a house together, but we never really married. We had separate bank accounts, separate cars, separate friends, and often separate vacations. He never added my name to the truck or the house in Golden, and I didn't really care. I had my own investments. We enjoyed the same movies, books, and traveling, but that was about the end of our sharing.

I don't blame him for the failure of our marriage. When my brother-in-law died, I was on the plane to Virginia before I even mentioned anything to Monte. I didn't think to ask Monte to attend the services in South Dakota when my sister died. I left while he was at work. He often went home for the holidays without me, and when his sister-in-law died, I didn't go with him to Missouri.

By 2008, my marriage was falling apart. I had my libido in check and thought it would be for the rest of my life. What I didn't count on was my husband's waning libido. By the eighth year of our marriage, we had utterly stopped touching each other, not even the occasional hug. He thought my writing novels was silly, and I felt his camping in the same spot every time was annoying.

To avoid the inevitable, I buried myself in my job. Unfortunately, in 2009 the entertainment industry changed. The entertainers chose to no longer be employees. I was no longer able to protect or train the entertainers as I once had. Dancing is like professional sports; it is a short-term career that can leave a person broken in many ways. The company still offers scholarships to entertainers so they can leave the industry with a secure future.

This was a bad place to be, but I hope I was some inspiration to the lost souls who passed my way. I'm still friends with many male and female employees who have moved on to a better life. I'm proud to see how far they have come from the days of dancing, bartending, or spinning tunes.

As time passed, I was promoted to an accounting and human resources desk job. The further I got away from working with the employees, the less I liked my job. I hated working with insurance and lawsuits. I didn't find counting money and tracing credit cards fulfilling.

Back in 2010, I found something in Monte's lunch box that led me to believe he was having an affair. While I was hurt, it explained so much. On his 60th birthday, I suggested meeting him at his favorite bar after work. I felt something was wrong when he told me to call before showing up. I never confronted him, but I began to pull away. I was lonely. I missed being treated like someone special. I wanted someone who wanted me as a wife, not a roommate.

I spent many hours with Lois, discussing everything, including my marriage. It was about this time that Lois was baptized. I was proud of her and gave her a small gold cross. Something was tickling the back of my mind, but I was not ready to go back to church. How could I explain my job? I didn't believe I could quit. Like the entertainers, I got used to the money. Now I wish I had talked more about her conversion. Instead of this bringing us closer, I felt it pulled us apart. Had I known anything about the Bible, I would have tried to save my marriage, but these things were not to be learned for several years.

❧📖❦

Frustrated, I wrote a long letter to Monte in the spring of 2011 explaining why I wanted a divorce. I didn't give the letter to him until a friend forced my hand by telling him I was planning to ask for a divorce. Once it was in the open, the divorce was amicable and only took a couple of months. We are still friends but not as close as we once were.

Also, in the summer of 2011, I published book two of the trilogy I was writing. I was a marketing novice, and social media was essential to advertising. I hired Lois for my marketing. She made my website and opened a Facebook page.

It was so easy to find old friends. Brad and I had kept in touch throughout the years, and he introduced me to a Facebook Page called "You know you're from Sioux Falls/Brandon if…."

This page was a great way of connecting with old high school friends and letting them know I was writing books. One of the people I reconnected with was Kevin. He was a senior when I was a Junior at Brandon Valley High. We had a couple of classes together but ran in different circles, so we didn't know each other well. Over the subsequent year, Kevin and I became close friends. He lived in North Carolina, and I lived in Colorado, so most of our time together was by Facebook, phone, or text.

Kevin was what I considered a highly religious man. He had been a pastor of his church when he lived in Florida, and he often posted biblical messages. We spent hours on the phone talking about the Bible and Christianity. I had so many questions. I didn't know if I was asking questions just to talk to him or if it was leading to something else. At this juncture of my life, I was anti-organized religion. I'd broken every vow I'd ever made, and I was thinking about another man before the ink was dry on my divorce papers.

In 2012, Kevin was still married. As our relationship changed and became sexually intimate, I was increasingly more uncomfortable dating a married man. I was uncomfortable but not uncomfortable enough to stop. Like any addiction, neither one of us could walk away. I was ashamed of my actions but didn't think about praying for relief or turning away.

Over the past forty years, I invested vast amounts of time, energy, and money in the Libertarian Party, including co-producing the 2008 National Libertarian Convention. I served as a national delegate to nearly every National Convention.

Kevin was an active member of the Libertarian Party in North Carolina, and we met in person at the 2012 LP National Convention. We met several times after that.

In early 2013, his wife discovered the affair and kicked him out of the house. He filed for divorce and moved to Colorado. By the autumn of 2013, we were living together. I was ashamed of what I'd done. I believe my dating a married man drove another small wedge between Lois and me.

❧📖❧

In 2015 I met someone in the LP who was intelligent, energetic, and well-spoken. After a year of seeing Caryn function on the state board, I learned she wasn't healthy. She displayed ruthless narcissistic tendencies. She relentlessly interpreted the Bylaws and Libertarian constitution to her own benefit. She bullied coworkers into getting her way or being the center of attention, seeking power with every action.

When Kevin Moved to Colorado, he and I became a formidable team. Aside from traveling across the state to work outreach booths as outreach director and fundraising director, we both ran for public office. Kevin ran for State House in 2016, 2018, 2020, and 2022. I ran for State Senate in 2012, 2016, and 2020. In 2018 and 2022, I was the Libertarian candidate for Lt. Governor.

When Caryn ran for a seat on the Libertarian National Committee in 2018, I didn't vote for her. When people asked why I wasn't supporting her, I told them I didn't think she was a good candidate, but I didn't go into specifics.

Her husband, the delegation chair, told Caryn I didn't vote for her. The next day I received a scathing email accusing me of betraying her and damaging Colorado. This would be the first of many attacks against my character and friends.

When she ran for re-election in 2020, I ran an active campaign against her, hoping others would see the negative traits I saw in her and had been subjected to.

Negative campaigning is mean and nasty. I copied remarks Caryn had made on Facebook and made awful memes about her obsession with Robert's Rules of Order and our Bylaws. I never believed myself capable of doing and saying such horrible things. I truly felt terrible after it was all over. I learned from this experience; hate begets hate. She doubled down, and her attacks on me became more blatant and direct.

After the election, I removed the anti-Caryn campaign webpage and kept clear of her and her husband. I tried not to follow Caryn's antics on Facebook because it only angered me.

❧ 📖 ❦

I retired from the club in December of 2019, right before COVID-19 hit. Little did I know how my life was going to change. I had planned to work as a part-time consultant. I was offered a decent hourly rate and had a couple of projects lined up. When the shutdown came, the club could only afford to keep me on for a couple of small projects.

In September 2020, Kevin and I packed up our camper and began a thirty-two-state tour of the eastern United States. We had planned to be home by Thanksgiving, but the country was so beautiful that we didn't come home until the end of January 2021. By then, we both could claim to have visited all fifty states.

While visiting North Carolina, we stopped at the Billy Graham Museum and Library in Charlotte, NC. Billy Graham was known for his large outdoor rallies and broadcast radio and television sermons. He and Martin Luther King Jr held a joint revival in New York City in 1957.

Reading about his life and listening to one of his calls to Jesus moved me to tears, and I began to question my (dis)belief in God. Since we first talked, Kevin has always answered my questions about God and the Bible. This was odd because I had never thought much about Christianity before meeting him.

In November, we visited Kevin's friends Sharon and Roy. They were part of Kevin's small group when he was a pastor in Florida.

We were spending Thanksgiving in Florida, our camper parked in their driveway. When they got home from spending time with their family, we were treated to delightful leftovers and great conversation. On Sunday, they tuned in to the live broadcast of the service from Church by the Glades. I was transfixed. I felt like everything Pastor David Hughes said was directed toward me and my life at that precise moment. I began praying in earnest over the next few months, asking if this was a call to return to a faith I never understood. I found myself asking God if this was why Kevin and his family were brought into my life.

The circumstances of our meeting were so very wrong that I couldn't fathom God approving or being behind it. Of course, God never condones evil, but that doesn't mean he can't use it for good. When Joseph was sold into slavery by his brothers, God orchestrated Joseph's progress so he could save his brothers years later.

Knowing that Kevin and I were both ending our current relationships and would be moving on to new partners, somehow, God managed to bring us together.

Once we were home in February, we got involved with the Libertarian Party Bylaws and produced the 2021 State Convention. We worked tirelessly over the next several months. We worked at the convention from May 21st through May 23rd, and both contracted COVID-19.

The Storm

1 Peter 4
*12Dear friends, don't be surprised at the fiery trials you
are going through, as if something strange were happening
to you. 13 Instead, be very glad—for these trials make
you partners with Christ in his suffering, so that you will
have the wonderful joy of seeing his glory when it is
revealed to all the world.*
[NLT]

I didn't realize we were sick because the results of the convention so disheartened me. The Meses faction hijacked the convention with all new members and overturned everything we tried to accomplish. Everyone previously active in the party was kicked to the curb, and an entirely new board was elected, including Caryn and her husband. Not only did all nine persons lose their place on the State Board, none of the regular activists, including Kevin and I, were selected to be national delegates. I was so depressed; I didn't realize I was sick.

I had a bad headache the second week of June and was exhausted. Kevin started showing more flu-like symptoms. After about six days, I started feeling better, but Kevin worsened. By Sunday, June 13th, his breathing was labored. I asked him to go to the hospital, but he refused.

On Monday, I was more insistent. He finally agreed to let me take him to the hospital.

Parker Adventist Hospital is less than five miles from our house, so that was the emergency room of choice. On the way to the hospital, he appeared to have a seizure. His eyes were open, and he was still breathing rapidly but wasn't conscious. As I pulled up to the emergency room, he wasn't breathing, he had no pulse, and his vacuous eyes stared into space.

I ran inside and grabbed the first person I saw. It turned out to be a receptionist for the

Children's Hospital, but she radioed for help. Two large men were able to get Kevin out of the car and onto the gurney. One of the men jumped on top of the gurney and started giving Kevin CPR. As I watched them wheel him into the hospital, a man straddling his chest, trying to bring him back to life, I fell to my knees and prayed to God. All I wanted was a little more time, a chance to say goodbye.

I parked the car and went inside. Because of COVID, I wasn't allowed in the emergency room. They directed me to a private waiting room. Shortly after, a minister came in to see how I was doing. By this time, I was completely numb. We talked about Kevin and a little about our families.

The time dragged on as we waited to see if Kevin would pull through. The minister prayed with me even though I told him I wasn't religious.

He said, "God doesn't care."

When he went to check on Kevin, I called Guy, Kevin's brother, and my sisters to let them know what had happened. I was a wreck, so I don't remember the details.

When the priest returned to tell me Kevin had been revived, I felt something powerful in the room. They restarted Kevin's heart and put him on a ventilator. I thanked God in earnest. The timing was so critical that I had to believe it could only have been Divine intervention.

I hurried outside to meet Guy, but when we got back, we still weren't allowed to see Kevin.

My sisters came to the hospital and waited to see if there were any changes. Hours later, he was sent up to ICU. He tested positive for COVID, so he was quarantined.

The doctor met with me and said Kevin suffered kidney and liver damage due to cardiac arrest. The EMTs spent a lot of time trying to revive him, so brain damage from loss of oxygen was possible. Kevin's heart was beating on its own, but he was unresponsive.

Not being able to see Kevin or do anything to help, Guy and I went home. We sat in the house and stared off into space for several hours. I sent a Facebook message to Kevin's daughters, Kelly and Kerry. They responded with their phone numbers within minutes, but I was too distraught to speak to anyone. I responded by text with the little information I knew. Because I had promised to take care of their dad, part of me felt I had failed them by letting Kevin get so sick.

Monday night was a blur. I waited all night for a call from the nurse to tell me how Kevin was doing. The call never came, and I was a complete mess. I don't believe I slept that night.

Tuesday morning, I got a call from the hospital saying they needed Kevin's insurance information, Living Will, and Medical Directive. I took the paperwork and his Medical Power of Attorney to the hospital. The emergency room let me make what decisions were needed on

Monday, but they needed it in writing now that he was in ICU.

Late Tuesday afternoon, the attending doctor called to talk to me about Kevin's Living Will, specifically his "Do Not Resuscitate" clause. As his medical Power of Attorney, I was overriding Kevin's wishes. According to his Will, I shouldn't have allowed them to give him CPR or insert the ventilator.

The doctor told me they took him off the adrenaline drip for his heart, which was still beating on its own. They had him in an induced coma so he wouldn't fight the ventilator. They also cooled him to prevent brain damage. The doctor wanted me to understand that due to the severity of the cardiac arrest, Kevin probably wouldn't recover and could remain in a vegetative state if he woke from the coma. He offered to make him comfortable and remove the tubes that were keeping him alive.

I felt dizzy and short of breath. This wasn't a decision I could make alone. After hanging up, I spoke with Kelly and Kerry by phone, but my mind was short-circuiting, and I couldn't find the words. I wanted to pray, but having never been a practicing Christian, I didn't know what to say.

Later that day, Kelly sent me the following prayer. Reading the words helped me focus my thoughts.

"Jesus, I come to your gates with thanksgiving and praise. I thank you that you are our perfect healer. I praise you that you have given us the power and authority to bring heaven to earth. So, I pray right now in the mighty name of Jesus that you invade Kevin's body and breathe life into it. Speak to all organs and command them back to proper function in the name of Jesus. Speak to oxygen levels back to 98%, blood and kidneys back to normal. I thank you, Jesus, that right now you are working even when we can't see it. We speak life over Kevin. Thank you, Jesus, that this will just be a part of his testimony of your healing power. We thank you, Holy Spirit for being in that place with him. May he know and feel your presence with him right now. I pray for each family member that your peace that surpasses all understanding be upon them. May they remember Jesus is greater in them, than the devil of this world. I thank you that they are geared up in your armor and no weapon formed against them will prosper. May they know and feel you are surrounding them and Kevin. Thank you, LORD, for your constant faithfulness, goodness, love, and mercy. We praise you in the storm. Amen."

Before going to bed, I thought I should let his friends and family know what was happening. I posted the information on Facebook and tagged him so his friends would know.

As a private person, posting my feelings was well out of my comfort zone. Funny memes, cats, dogs, and photos of travel were safe, but nothing too personal and never my innermost thoughts. Below is the first post I made updating friends and family on Kevin's condition.

"Most people know I don't share personal information about my life on Facebook, but yesterday, the love of my life had a massive heart attack on the way to the hospital. He is in ICU, but the prognosis is bleak. He is on life support now. His daughter, Kerry, and his granddaughter Erowyn will be here tomorrow, but the hospital is not letting anyone see him. Covid. I never knew I could cry so much."

☙📖❧

I walked around in a daze all Wednesday morning. There was nothing I could do but worry and pray. Kevin's daughter, Kelly, managed to get through to the doctor by phone in the afternoon, and he sounded encouraged.

Kelly reported that Kevin had far exceeded the doctor's expectations. The COVID-induced lung injury resulted in big clots in Kevin's lungs. The clots blocked the outflow of the heart, which caused organ failure and cardiac arrest. She said that Kevin had another large clot which nearly caused another arrest on Monday night. They found another small clot on the tricuspid and started him on heparin to address it. He was initially on 100% oxygen but down to 40-50% by Wednesday. They moved him from the prone position to his back, which he tolerated well. They lowered the sedation slightly, and he started moving around. That was a good sign. The doctor couldn't make any predictions until Kevin cleared the sedation but said, "he is headed in the right direction fairly quickly."

I read and re-read Kelly's post a dozen times. It gave me a feeling of hope. Her report was much better than my last conversation with the doctor, who had offered to make Kevin comfortable until he passed.

There is no medical explanation for the rapid turnaround. I attribute it to God's goodness and to everyone who lifted a prayer when I couldn't find the words myself. I prayed that this trajectory would continue and that there would be no signs of brain damage. I praised God!

Kerry and her daughter, Erowyn, arrived from New Hampshire late Wednesday night. Their plane was delayed two hours, but even so, that little five-year-old was in good spirits. I was glad to see them. We talked a bit about how we would split up Kevin's belongings, primarily musical instruments, if things worsened. I'm the type of person who tries to stay busy when faced with emotional tragedy. Staying active keeps me from having to face emotional pain. I was trying to make peace with losing him, button down my feelings, and make logical choices.

When my sister, Debbie, passed away, I spent hours planning the service and attending to my siblings. It was days before the impact of her passing registered. I can appear cold and heartless in the face of tragedy, but that's my coping mechanism.

Leaving the airport, I was barely keeping it together. Kerry was so encouraging. The word Zen came to mind. Even in the worse situations, Kerry was (and still is!) so calm, full of love, and 100% real.

We got back to the house after midnight. I didn't sleep much that night. All I could do was cry.

❧📖❧

They lifted the quarantine on Thursday. ICU would only allow one visitor at a time, but I was so grateful to be able to see him. Before going to visit, Kevin's brother, Guy, and I got a COVID test. Unfortunately, Guy tested positive and was confined to his house for the next ten days. I thanked God that I tested negative and could be with Kevin. I packed small speakers, his old iPhone for music, pictures of his family, and his mother's bible, then raced to the hospital.

My last vision of him in the car had been horrifying; he had no life in his eyes and no movement in his chest. Seeing him in the ICU with a dozen tubes, wires, and medications running into his body wasn't much better. His legs moved a little, but he didn't respond when the nurse asked him to squeeze her hand.

The artwork around the hospital was so hopeful and calming. I don't know the denomination, but the brass statue depicting Jesus with children, the lion, and the lamb was the perfect inspiration for a broken heart. There were several paintings of Jesus in different situations. In one, Jesus has his hand on a doctor's shoulder while performing surgery. Just looking at those paintings made me feel like Jesus was right there with me.

Children weren't allowed in the hospital during those COVID days, so I went downstairs to stay with Erowyn while Kerry spent time with her dad. Seeing her sitting in the lap of Jesus is a memory that will stay with me forever.

After Kerry and Erowyn went home, the doctor stopped by. He reminded me that Kevin may have suffered brain damage from the cardiac arrest and the initial seizure, if that's what it was, before his heart stopped.

Kevin had a couple of these episodes in the past, but he refused to go to a doctor to have it checked out. The first time it happened, I called 911. By the time they got to the house, Kevin was back to normal. All his vital signs were within normal range, and the EMTs couldn't say what was wrong without an MRI. He blacked out again on the couch a couple of months later but recovered quickly. He still refused to see a doctor, but I told his daughters about the seizures because I feared he wouldn't recover one day. He didn't have insurance at the time, so I didn't press it. The next time he blacked out, we were in the camper. It only lasted about five seconds. In the spring of 2021, he blacked out again at home while entertaining friends. I tried to get him to a doctor, but he didn't think it was serious.

He has always been on the blackout side of these incidents. I'm the one who watches the light go out of his eyes. I can't tell you how truly frightening it is to watch someone die.

Back in the ICU, I wasn't sure he knew I was with him. The sedation was wearing off, and his eyes opened. I kept talking non-stop, trying to stay positive. His eyes followed me sometimes, so he could likely see at this point.

I stayed until visiting hours were over. On the way home, I thanked God for giving me another day with Kevin. This was my chance to have closure and to say goodbye. Most families don't get that chance, and I was eternally grateful to see life in Kevin's eyes again.

As I said earlier, I was never one to pray unless I was in crisis. This night, I prayed a very different prayer. I realized, for the first time in my life, how very blessed I am. It was like my heart was swelling in my chest. I now understood gratitude, something I had never genuinely experienced before.

Kerry had dinner ready when I came in. I hadn't thought about eating all day, so I was quite hungry. It was nearly 9:00 pm, and Erowyn was asleep. Kerry and I talked for a few minutes, but I was exhausted. That night, I got down on my knees and prayed for strength to get through this trial. I also asked for a sign of what I should do about Kevin's DNR. (*Do Not Resuscitate* directive).

≈📖≈

On Friday, I woke up at about 5:00 am. I got down on my knees again and asked for everything I had asked before, but this time, I appreciated the gifts I had already received. I was thankful I had Guy's support and Kerry was with me. Mostly, I was grateful that God chose to give me another day with Kevin.

Visiting hours started at 6:00 am, and I was waiting at the front door by ten minutes 'til. When I got to Kevin's room, the nurse said he had a calm night. I sat next to his bed and thumbed through his mother's bible, hoping to find comfort in God's Word. His mother had made hundreds of notes in the margins and circled many verses. I didn't understand the notes any more than the original text. For me, The Bible was like reading Shakespeare; the language was so foreign.

Because God had saved Kevin's life, I felt I needed to understand more about God and his Word. The first verse I opened to and read was underlined.

Isaiah 40:31
But they that wait upon the LORD shall renew their strength; they shall mount up with wings as eagles; they shall run, and not be weary; and they shall walk, and not faint.
(NKJV)

As I read the words, I realized this was the verse on Kevin's favorite mug and on a model sailboat he had on his desk. Tears streamed down my face. It was like a personal message to me to not give up hope for Kevin's recovery.

The nurses changed shifts around 7:00 am. They come in together to do a neural test. This morning, Kevin opened his eyes when the nurse called his name. She asked him to squeeze her hand but didn't respond. He might have wiggled his fingers on his right hand and maybe his toes, but we couldn't be sure. His stare was blank. His oxygen was still 50% machine provided.

Morning rounds began around 10:00 am. Kevin's doctors and nurses gathered outside his room to review his prognosis and medications. His pulmonary doctor said he was surprised by Kevin's rapid recovery. He stated that only .04% of patients survive a cardiac arrest like Kevin's.

Even fewer survive when they suffer a cardiac arrest in a car in the hospital parking lot. The doctor said, "don't believe what you see on television; they would have you believe 90% come back. This past Monday, four patients coded, and Kevin was the only one of the four to survive."

Hearing this, I got my first genuine touch of God's hand. As dire as Kevin's circumstances were, I felt a sudden wave of peace. It was almost joy. I knew, without any doubt, that God had chosen Kevin for a purpose. He wasn't out of the woods yet, but I relaxed for the first time since bringing him to the hospital five days ago.

Later that morning, the doctors tried to wake him up (cut off the sedative), but Kevin's heart went crazy. They upped the sedative dosage and restarted the Amiodarone drip. Before leaving, the doctor said he would try to wake Kevin again tomorrow. That was the first step needed to take him off the ventilator. The ventilator was primarily assisting. He tended to hyperventilate, and his heart would get erratic. Fortunately, he reacted well to the medication. Kevin breathed independently for several hours, but I could see he was in pain. It was so hard to watch. Sometimes, noises would make him open his eyes, but he wasn't responding to commands. There was a chance he would come off the ventilator on Saturday, which would at least reduce his pain.

He made minor improvements throughout the day. By noon, I could tell he understood what I was saying. I wasn't sure he recognized me. Most of the time, he just stared into space.

The nurse's afternoon rounds included a neural test and a blood draw. Kevin's kidneys weren't where they needed to be, but there had been no additional deterioration. His ability to wiggle toes and fingers or squeeze her hand had not changed. He opened his eyes at the sound of his name, but he couldn't follow her finger. His oxygen was at 50% on the ventilator. They took him off the Amiodarone drip again, and he seemed to be doing okay.

As I left for the night, I realized the most challenging part of praying was feeling the Lord had already done so much by restarting Kevin's heart. I had asked for more time with him, and my prayer was answered. I had been given another day with Kevin. I was so thankful. Every minute with him was a blessing.

When I got home from the hospital at 8:30 pm, Kerry had dinner ready. I probably wouldn't have eaten anything if she hadn't made dinner. I am forever grateful to her. Kelly would be arriving on Saturday. I found myself thanking God for the simplest of thing, like having room in my home for these incredible women.

Kelly posted on Facebook, sharing her thoughts with her friends and church. I found comfort in reading her memories of her dad and her prayers. Hundreds of loving comments followed these posts. The outpouring of love from his family, friends, and many people I don't know, helped me sleep through the night.

Psalm 27:13
I would have lost heart, unless I had believed that I would see the goodness of the LORD in the land of the living.
(NKJV)

❧📖❧

Saturday morning I was waiting for the doors to open at 6:00 am. Gone are the days when you could stay in the hospital all night. Maybe it's better that I went home and slept. That also let the nurses do what they needed to without me questioning every procedure. The doctors and nurses at Adventist were terrific. They never seemed to mind having me underfoot.

He was awake and focused when I entered his room. He knew what I was saying and even tried to talk. My relief was overwhelming. I was so excited, so hopeful; each little thing meant his brain was intact. When I told him I couldn't remember the code to get into his phone, he tried to laugh as well as he could with all those tubes in his throat. The improvement was dramatic.

He did considerably better on his neural test. He was able to squeeze the nurse's hand and wiggle his toes. He still couldn't do much with his left hand or foot, and there was a tiny bit of sag on the left side of his face. The doctor said his left-side weakness might have been caused by a lack of oxygen during his heart failure, much like a stroke.

They put a PICC line into his heart. He had one in his groin, but they moved it to his arm. There was less chance of infection with the more direct line.

Later that morning, the nurse tried to wean him off the ventilator. They shut off the pressure that opens his lungs to see if Kevin could keep breathing.

He breathed on his own for about an hour before needing an oxygen boost, and the nurse upped the pressure.

The doctor and I talked about taking him off the ventilator again. The longer a person is on it, the less chance of surviving without permanent damage. This was a huge decision to make. If he couldn't breathe on his own, he would die. If they reinserted the ventilator, his chances of survival would be significantly reduced.

Kevin's directive clearly stated, "no artificial life support." I was utterly overcome. I knew Kevin would hate me if I condemned him to a wheelchair and artificial life support for the rest of his life. We had had many long discussions about this when we filled out our Living Wills.

Kelly was on an airplane, and Kerry left the decision to me. I couldn't make that decision alone. I needed help. I prayed; no, let's be honest, I paced and begged God for a sign telling me if I should override Kevin's Living Will.

Kevin woke up a few minutes after my crying/pacing/praying bout. He seemed very aware. I explained to him what was going to happen that afternoon. He nodded that he understood they would be removing the ventilator that was forcing him to breathe. Then I asked him about his Living Will, specifically about putting the ventilator back in if he couldn't survive without it.

Twice, he shook his head, "no" don't put it back in.

I reminded him that if he couldn't breathe on his own, he would die, and I asked again if he understood. He nodded.

I can't tell you how hard that was. I had asked God for a clear sign of what to do, and you couldn't get any clearer than that. I broke down in tears again. My heart was breaking from the fear of losing him, and knowing he was ready to die.

It was at that moment, sitting on the couch in Kevin's room, that I placed it all in God's hands. Speaking only to Him I said, *"Thank you for the extra days you have given me with Kevin. Thank you for your guidance through this tough decision. There is nothing I can do now. It's all up to you, Lord."*

It might sound crazy, but I immediately felt a profound sense of peace. The weight was lifted off my shoulders. It was as if I had nothing to worry about, which didn't make sense considering my circumstances. That was when I knew, without any doubt, that God was carrying me, and with God, I could face anything.

Kelly arrived at the hospital shortly after I told the doctor we wouldn't reinsert the ventilator if his breathing failed. I was glad to have her there. Thankfully, by this time, it was too late on Saturday to complete the procedure.

As much as I wanted to see that monster out of him, I was happy to wait another day or two. Since he had indicated that he didn't want to be intubated again, the doctors were being conservative, giving him the best possible chance to survive.

They told me that once he was off the ventilator, if the extubating went well, they could do an MRI to determine better if he had suffered a stroke in combination with everything else.

❧📖☙

Kelly said she hadn't been prepared to see her dad in this condition and prayed that no one else would have to see a loved one suffer like this. I agreed. I didn't take any pictures because I never wanted to remember how frightening this was. One of the nurses told us they'd seen so many COVID patients who were worse. I can't even begin to fathom. We prayed for the millions of people walking around with the scars of seeing their loved ones in this situation.

Shortly after, Kerry came to get Kelly and had a short visit with her dad. While Kerry spent time with her dad, Kelly prayed with me. Prayer was foreign to me. I was grateful to have her words of love and faith. I don't know what I would have done without the support of Kevin's daughters. Every day I had with them was a gift.

When I got home, the girls had supper ready. I had a little more time to talk to them about their faith. Kelly is a born-again Evangelical Christian. Kerry is Buddhist. I could clearly see how their faith made them peaceful and loving. Years ago, I took a college course on religion that included Hinduism and Buddhism. While the philosophies were interesting, the past week's events assured me that Jesus is unquestionably real.

The Holy Spirit was guiding me through every step of this ordeal. Those who believe understand what I was feeling. I had never felt this before and could never have imagined how it would change me. All my priorities completely changed. I wanted to know everything about

God, and to hold on to this connection with something greater than me, this sense of peace. I was exhausted but so grateful.

᪥📖᪥

By Father's Day, Kevin had been intubated for six days. He was alert when I came in. I told him how much I loved him and that no matter what happened, I would forever belong to God.

Kelly, Kerry, and I traded off, giving each of us a chance to say all the important things you say to someone when you're not sure you will get another chance.

While Kevin slept or the girls were with him, I thanked everyone for their love, prayers, and help through this tough time. I sent a private note to his family, letting everyone know that the ventilator would soon be removed.

Everyone had to leave the room so they could take the ventilator out. I didn't want to see the procedure anyway. The doctor said he probably wouldn't be able to talk for a couple of days even if the strokes hadn't damaged his motor skills. They would know in about an hour if the removal was successful. Life's lessons can be brutal, but I still thank God for His endless love and mercy.

Kelly and I paced the waiting room, praying, but I was torn in my prayers. It felt so selfish to want Kevin to recover. I didn't want to live without him, but I couldn't help thinking of all the other families who had lost loved ones. I stumbled over asking God to heal people. While I know God can heal them, I don't know if that is in His plan. I just prayed over and over that God would keep Kevin breathing.

About 30 minutes later, they let me into his room. The first thing Kevin said was, "I love you." I burst into tears and thanked the Lord. I can still feel the goosebumps today as I write this story.

Kevin still had a long road ahead, but I believed the worst of it might be behind us. He was a miracle man—one of God's many miracles.

I ran down the hall to tell Kelly that her father had survived the extubating. One of the nurses stopped me to see if I was okay. I was sobbing but so very happy. I'm sure she thought something terrible had happened.

I said, "he said; I love you." She must have understood because she smiled at me and said, "I'm glad."

While this is my story, Kelly's words were so eloquent that I want to share them. You can see how much her faith strengthened me during these demanding days.

Kelly's Facebook Post: June 20
"HE'S OFF THE VENT! All praise hands going up here! The nurse said, "He is doing "good." Their definition of good is much different than mine. He still looks so pitiful to me, and he has such a long way to go, but I know he

still very much has the will to fight through this. Michele is with him now.

I saw him, and he was able to say, "I love you." The rest of his speech was garbled, so I'm praying fervently that his ability to speak returns. I prayed big, bold prayers during the extubating and begged God to let him go peacefully if he was not going to be able to have a life where he could speak and communicate and/or eat. Trusting in the Lord in this. It is beyond difficult to feel the weight of responsibility for these decisions. Thankful that Michele and Kerry are here and that we've been able to talk through it together, AND that he's been somewhat responsive and indicative of his wishes.

Keep praying for those lungs to continue to heal, for his breathing to become easy (this could take months due to the extent of the covid lung injury), and especially pray for his brain. Increased responsiveness, improved speech, strength on the left side, etc. I can't even think clearly enough to pray all the things. Thankful that God knows his every need."

֍ 📖 ֍

Kevin had been hospitalized for a week, and so much of my life had changed. That first week was mostly a blur. Each day I was up before the alarm and asleep within ten minutes of my head hitting the pillow. Anyone who knows me knows I have insomnia most nights, and I walk around half-asleep for the first two hours after I drag myself out of bed.

The morning after the extubating, the nurse who had been with Kevin when he was admitted came in to apologize for not calling me back. She told me she didn't remember that I wanted her to call me until she got home. She had been too busy with his care. She felt terrible and couldn't imagine how worried I'd been. She then told me four people coded (had a cardiac arrest) that day, and Kevin was the only one who survived.

I could only attribute this to God. I realized then; He must have had a reason for saving Kevin when those other families lost their loved ones. I was flooded with guilt yet incredibly grateful. *Thank you, God, for this gift. I am a true believer now.*

The doctor who saw Kevin the day he was admitted said the CT showed some changes to the back part of the brain. This might impact his vision and motor functions. The markers could be due to a stroke or Posterior Reversible Encephalopathy Syndrome. (PRES is a disorder of acute onset neurological symptoms due to reversible subcortical vasogenic brain edema). In plain language, that's swelling in the brain, much like a concussion. It is something that tends to resolve over time. They would monitor the spots with more scans over time.

Kevin didn't do well with his peripheral vision in either eye, but the left was notably worse than the right. They did another X-ray of his lungs. We had hoped to have an MRI scheduled by the end of the week. His oxygen needed to be stable enough to lay flat for forty-five minutes in an MRI machine. He was currently on 40 Liters of oxygen, and he needed to get down to 6 Liters before moving out of ICU.

Each day, I thanked God for the loving staff and this hospital.

An admissions counselor stopped by to talk about moving Kevin to a rehab facility in the next week. It was a nightmare; one day, he was on the brink of death, and the next, he was planning to move to a rehabilitation center.

This was Kelly's last full day in Colorado. She was scheduled to fly to North Carolina on Tuesday. I was so thankful she could make this trip and have quality time with her dad.

Kerry and Erowyn would be staying with me for another month. I was happy to give his daughters as much time as possible with their dad, but to be honest, I went a little crazy if I couldn't see what was happening to Kevin moment by moment.

While Kelly and Kerry were visiting with their dad, I tried to make sense of our finances. Until today, our bills were the last thing on my mind. All my focus was on getting Kevin through this.

While traveling in 2020, Kevin and I put everything online using Kevin's Online banking account. When he got sick, he couldn't give me his passwords. I couldn't get into his banking accounts or his phone. Trying to get our bills switched back to paper billing was a nightmare. I mailed a copy of our notarized Power of Attorney to all our accounts, but it would be months before I could get a handle on our finances.

Through this, I practiced my patience and my praying skills.

I was so relieved by the success of removing the ventilator I barely remember Monday and Tuesday. When Kelly asked him if he remembered what had happened, he said no.

She said, "That's probably a good thing. We're glad you're still here."

He said, "I wish I was someplace else."

"Touché."

I was so blessed to have him come so far in seven days. I knew this was a miracle, all because of God's mercy and our friend's prayers. God is so good. I know Jesus never promises to work things out the way we want, but He had chosen to answer every prayer we lifted.

The doctor said it could take a couple of days before Kevin could swallow solids. I hoped he would be motivated and not frustrated with the process. The speech consult went well. He was on high-flow oxygen, so while the therapist thought he was swallowing well, they wanted to wait on liquids until his oxygen needs reduce. She explained how his nutrition went through his nasal tube but expected that he would be eating soon.

She said, "You need to work for it."

His reply was, "I want a steak."

The nurse did some mouth swabs so that his mouth wasn't dry and gave him some lip balm. It was pomegranate flavored, and she apologized for the weird flavor.

He said, "it's okay. I like pomegranates."

That's my Kevin in a nutshell.

Gratefully, he was allowed a couple of ice chips every hour. He constantly begged for ice chips, and he would pout when I told him he needed to wait a bit longer.

Kevin was so sweet to all the doctors and nurses, even those who had later been assigned to other patients stopped in to say hello.

While visiting Kevin, Kelly talked about their history with musical theater and instructed him to use his loud and proud voice.

He loudly said, "I'M LOUD, and I'M PROUD," which made the nurse giggle.

Kevin said, "Loud, so they can hear me in the back row."

Kelly said, "and enunciation,"

He said, "So they can understand me in the back row."

His voice was weak, but Kevin continued to work on his projection and speaking loudly. To build his diaphragm, he practiced saying "I love Michele" as loud as he could. I could feel my face flush, but I was so glad to hear the words.

He had a flutter tube to breathe into ten times every hour and improved drastically in three hours. Kevin was ready and willing to do the hard work even when he wasn't asked.

The chaplain came in and prayed with Kevin while Kerry was with him. He really loved that. His daughters mean the world to him. He won't sleep if they are in the room for fear of missing time with them. I'm so glad they could be here. I am so very thankful for every answered prayer.

We continued to pray for increased mobility, stronger lungs, and that he could eat steak soon. Although he was still a little confused, we prayed there would be no long-term brain damage.

"Thank you, My Lord Jesus. All the glory for the multitude of miracles that have gotten us here goes to You and You alone!"

After the girls left, I sat with Kevin. He was exhausted. The physical therapists came in and helped him try to sit up. His chest hurt, and he couldn't breathe, so it was a short therapy session. While they were here, the therapists and I reviewed the house arrangements for his rehabilitation and home care. I needed a few things, but the main floor of the house has two bedrooms, his office, the dining room, and the kitchen. There are no stairs if he comes from the garage.

My sister, Bette, offered to let Kevin use our stepmother's old wheelchair. Before my father passed, he had a Hoveround electric chair, and Bette will also drop that off. Kevin would love it even if he doesn't need it.

I learned where the ice machine was and how to exercise Kevin's feet and legs. He also had hand exercises I did with him every hour.

That night I had a wonderful dinner with Kelly and Kerry. We were all feeling less stressed now that Kevin was breathing and talking and still had his sense of humor. His improvements over the last two days exceeded all our expectations.

⋙📖⋘

Tuesday morning, Kelly and I went to the hospital together. She would be going to the airport from the hospital. I wanted her to have as much time as possible with her dad. While she sat with Kevin, I made calls and worked on our finances.

My sister, Christine, worked in billing at Denver Health, so I called her, asking what kind of bills I should expect and my prospects for assistance. We discussed Medicare, Medicaid, and selling the house. I needed time to research my choices. I knew the bills were piling up with each day.

After Kelly left for the airport, I went in to visit Kevin. I was shocked at how much easier he was speaking. He was talking continuously. The difference between last night and this morning was significant and so encouraging. He still had trouble consistently identifying the year, though he knew where he was and what had happened to him over the last eight days.

His new practice sentence was, "I WANT MORE ICE!" Kelly told him to add a please at the end, and maybe the nurses would let him have a little extra. He was only allowed a few pieces every hour, which became his favorite treat.

His therapist said they would taper his oxygen down if Kevin kept his oxygen saturation at 95% or above. Then he could try some liquids or Jell-O. He got very excited at the mention of Jell-O.

His nurse said they don't see many patients who are as motivated as Kevin. He was doing his breathing exercises and usually did an extra one. For those who know Kevin, this didn't come as a surprise at all. The last thing you could ever call him is lazy. You can't be a first-chair trumpet player or run five marathons if you aren't willing to do the work.

After his nurse left, he asked me when he could walk and stand. I told him we would ask the physical therapist when she came in. Once he got going, I predicted it would be hard to slow him down. He was ready to go home.

His strength had improved on the left side from the previous day. He could briefly lift each leg and hold it up while resisting light pressure. It was encouraging. We were on the right track. It would take days to rebuild the muscles he lost.

I was just so thankful. Remembering the four patients who coded the day Kevin was brought in, my heart grieved for the families. I trusted that God would use every bit of this to do good things. He already had!

At about 9:40 pm, Kevin's heart went back into AFIB. They started him back on the Amiodarone drip, and the doctor said it might happen throughout his recovery. He didn't experience any discomfort or changes in breathing throughout. The alarm beeping was disconcerting. They said it could take hours to a day or two to get it settled entirely.

During rounds, the doctor was impressed that Kevin recognized him. Neurologically he seemed to be doing well. He still had some confusion or slow thinking, but hopefully, that would resolve over time. The Neurologist believed Kevin had a stroke, and it wasn't PRES syndrome.

The doctor said, "strokes are like real estate. It's all about location, location, location."

The area affected was apparently the least devastating and shouldn't affect his speech or motor skills extensively.

An MRI would be more conclusive. His peripheral vision was expected to improve, although Kevin may have some permanent blind spots. Most people learn to navigate those.

The chest X-ray from yesterday showed fluid and inflammation in Kevin's lungs. They started him on a new medication to help flush any fluid from the lungs.

The doctor mentioned that he could backslide during recovery, but I prayed hard against any regression. They adjusted his oxygen to 30 liters and, an hour later, lowered it again to 20 Liters. Lowering it twice in one day seemed like significant progress. It was hard to believe that he was on a ventilator two days ago. 6 Liters was the goal to get him out of the ICU. We all prayed for 6 Liters and praised the progress made in such a short time.

Based on how long he was on the ventilator, the therapist estimated twelve to sixteen weeks of rehabilitation. She said that rebuilding his muscles would take two to three weeks each day he was on the ventilator. He was disappointed at the length of time and tried to convince me he could do everything from home just like he did after his knee surgery. I felt sure he accepted that as a challenge and was determined to beat it. We set a goal of returning from the rehabilitation center before August first or five weeks. Regardless, this would be a long road to recovery even after he came home.

His kidneys continued to improve. They had sustained significant damage, so to be where he was on June twenty-second was great. I just focused on keeping him cheerful and encouraged. I let him know how many people loved him.

Adventist Hospital was comforting, like being held in a cocoon with Christ. I was thankful for all healthcare workers; it's truly a calling. God has uniquely enabled them to do the critical work they do each day.

❧📖❧

Oddly enough, I woke up most days without an alarm. I would drive to the hospital each day and spend the next fourteen hours sitting next to Kevin's bed. I've always avoided hospital visits, and I love to sleep late. I've never been one to display motherly nursing skills of any kind. I have always been able to find a million more important things to do to avoid an unpleasant task. I didn't recognize myself anymore. My entire focus was on Kevin's care.

On Wednesday, I got to the hospital at 5:45 am and waited for the doors to open. Unfortunately, this morning, Kevin didn't know why he was in the hospital or how he got there.

Once more, I explained everything he had been through over the last week and a half. Kevin remembered his birthday but still stumbled over the year he was born. He was better at moving his arms and legs but still weak. It isn't easy to get exercise when you have a dozen tubes running into your body.

I read some texts and emails from friends, which cheered him up. Kevin's sister, Gay texted this morning to say she and Dwayne would be visiting from the ninth through the twelfth of July. Kevin adores his little sister. I was probably pushing it, but it sounded like he might be home by then; he was recovering so fast.

Later in the afternoon, he returned to the heated high-flow oxygen again. He was lucid and speaking clearly. I had hoped the oxygen reader wasn't correctly attached because the alarms kept going off. The nurse changed it once, which was better for a while, but then the alarm started going off again. The doctor assured me this was not unusual, saying his oxygen would be up and down for some time. I must have driven the staff nuts with all my questions.

He did better on his neural test that afternoon. He knew the day of the week and the name of the hospital. Judging by how Kevin answered, I thought he was getting bored with the same questions twice a day.

A counselor from the discharge office came in and gave me some referrals for rehabilitation care and explained the next steps. The counselor was surprised by Kevin's quick recovery and said he could be out of the hospital as soon as next week. I Praised God because this was all His work. We chose a facility and made a therapy plan for bringing Kevin home.

On the drive home, my conversation with God was filled with thanksgiving. I don't know why my prayers were answered, but I will spend the rest of my life thanking Him for the gift he has given me.

❧📖❦

Thursday, June twenty-fourth, was day eleven of Kevin's hospitalization. Although his neural test went well, he still stumbled over the year. He was able to tell us his full name and location. He knew he was in the hospital for a heart attack from COVID and remembered that I drove him to the hospital. Just yesterday morning, he couldn't remember how he got to the hospital or why he was there.

We had a good conversation about the day I brought him to the hospital, and I asked if he wanted me to rub his feet.

"Always," he said.

During his speech therapy, he was able to eat some applesauce. Every day was another miracle.

Ten days earlier, I had brought him to the hospital without a heartbeat. Today he was playfully sassing the speech therapist about wanting green Jell-O.

The therapist ordered a barium test for the next day. Passing the barium test meant solid food and removal of the nasal feeding tube.

They decided to hold off on the MRI until the following Monday. Kevin's oxygen capacity wasn't quite stable enough to lie flat for the test. The MRI wouldn't have made any difference in his treatment, but it would have answered some essential questions. The doctor said he might move into a regular room tomorrow or Saturday.

When Kerry came to visit with her dad, I stayed with Erowyn. She played around the hospital's brass statues and showed me how to paint pictures with rainwater and feathers. I took a dozen photos to show Kevin since his granddaughter couldn't come inside.

After Kerry left, our friend Victoria stopped for a visit and stayed about forty-five minutes. Since we were limited to three visitors a day, Guy gave up his visitation with his brother.

A little later, a woman from Encompass Health rehabilitation hospital dropped off information. She said the average stay for COVID recovery was two weeks. She said it was reasonable to have Kevin home by August first or before. I was hoping for July fifteenth.

She spoke with Kevin's doctor and said they were expecting him to transfer to the rehabilitation hospital next week, roughly July first.

Unfortunately, Encompass Health would only allow two visitors a day, meaning Kerry and Guy would have to trade off their visitations.

During physical therapy, he could sit straighter but still couldn't hold his head up. The rehabilitation hospital would require four hours a day of therapy. The strength he had gained in just three days led me to believe he would be able to handle four hours of therapy by the following week.

Kevin was napping when the EMTs, who gave Kevin CPR that first day, stopped to see him. They said they were in the emergency room, talking with the doctor, and asked whatever happened to the guy they pulled out of the car. The doctor said, "He's doing fine. Go up and see him."

Seeing Kevin alert and smiling, they gave each other High-Fives. They were so sweet. I can't imagine how hard it is to lose someone; they must savor every win. They chatted with us for about 10 minutes. It did my heart good to see them so happy. Again, I praised the Lord for his mercy. This was a gift to many.

Later, when the regular doctor came in, Kevin asked if he was famous yet.

The doctor said, "yes."

Kevin said, "I'm feeling great, loved, and appreciative. God, in his mercy, is good. Praise the Lord."

One would think praising God a few dozen times a day would get old, but it didn't. I had no clear way to show God how truly thankful I was for the miracles I'd witnessed. I was overwhelmed with gratitude. I wanted to shout it from the rooftops. I settled for posting my joy and gratitude on Kevin's Facebook page every day.

Psalm 40
² He also brought me up out of a horrible pit, Out of the miry clay, and set my feet upon a rock, And established my steps. ³ He has put a new song in my mouth—Praise to our God; Many will see it and fear, and will trust in the LORD.
(NKJV)

❧📖❧

As joyful as Thursday was, Friday was a different story. That morning Kevin was extremely confused. Strangely, he couldn't remember the date or hospital name. He forgot several things he had answered right many times before. I decided to limit the time and number of visitors to myself, his brother Guy, and his daughter, Kerry. Kevin would never sleep if friends were in the room. He was always an entertainer and being on his deathbed wasn't stopping him. He saw several people yesterday, and I think it wore him out, like a child that gets overly tired and refuses to go to sleep.

At 10:00 am, Kevin was taken to radiology to test his swallowing. He wasn't the same when he came back from the barium test. I think all the moving around might have been too much for him. He was disappointed and depressed. He said he didn't think it went as well as they had hoped. The nurse confirmed he wasn't ready for solid food. They ordered another test for Monday. That meant his MRI would have to wait. He wasn't strong enough to do both in one day. That was okay with me because the results of the MRI wouldn't make any difference in his care, but having the feeding tube out would be a significant advancement. Guy came in today at 11:00, so I could go home to eat and let Kerry visit her dad for a while. Since the hospital was less than ten minutes away, it was easier for me to come home than to make Erowyn wait outside in the parking lot.

We were almost into a routine by this time, and I thanked God for every moment we had been given with Kevin. I was thankful it was summertime. I was thankful for blue skies and trees. I was thankful for every sunrise and every sunset. I was thankful Kerry could be with me. I was thankful we had more than one car, and I was thankful for Kevin's wonderful family.

When I returned to the hospital at about 2:00 pm, the nurse told me they would be moving Kevin out of ICU as soon as a bed opened in the Cardiac/Stroke unit. She thought it would be in the morning. This was a huge step forward.

The staff at Adventist is wonderful. Kevin had many different nurses and a couple of different doctors, but I couldn't be happier with their care.

I went through the usual exercises with Kevin. He could lift his legs and push against my hand, but his conversation didn't make sense. The muscle loss in Kevin's body was sad to see. I know from weightlifting how hard it is to recover as you get older. The liquid diet kept him alive, but solid food would do so much more for his strength.

By the end of the day, Kevin was showing signs of aphasia, the loss of using or understanding language. His speech was mostly nonsense, and some words were impossible to understand. I tried to get him to sleep, but he refused.

When I got home, I sent a Facebook update on his progress and thanked everyone for their prayers and love. I know this sounds crazy, but the love was so strong that I could feel it flowing into him daily. Hundreds of people sent prayers.

Kerry had dinner ready, and we made plans to bring Kevin home. She and Erowyn were planning to fly back to New Hampshire on Sunday. Their family was preparing to move back to the San Juan Islands, so they planned to be here for at least a week in August. Kerry said she would stay to help with Kevin's recovery while Jack works out living arrangements in Washington.

My prayers were once again full of thanks for the love of God and his Church. I finally understood. A church isn't a building. A church is a family of believers in Christ who love each other. God's love was palpable, like a warm blanket when I laid my head down to sleep. I can't explain it any other way. I have never felt so loved as in those days of Kevin's illness. It was truly humbling.

1 Corinthians 3
¹⁶Don't you know that you yourselves are God's temple and that God's Spirit dwells in your midst?
[NIV]

≈📖≈

I wasn't prepared for Saturday. The hospital staff restarted the Amiodarone drip when Kevin went into AFIB last night after I left. This morning Kevin showed signs of another heart attack, so they did another EKG and another ultrasound.

He was having a tough day. I thought he was having seizures again. He had trouble talking, and he was zoning out a lot. When this happens, you can't get his attention. He stares off without blinking, totally unconscious.

They started another EEG to follow his brain functions. He looked terrible with all those wires attached to his head and a big bandage holding it all in place.

He couldn't speak clearly and was losing ground quickly. He couldn't remember his name or the names of his daughters. I was glad Kelly didn't have to see this regression.

I wanted him to sleep, but he was fighting it. I think he was scared. Even if he couldn't say his name, he must have been aware enough to know something was dreadfully wrong. I wanted to help him, but I could only pray he would pull out of this new nightmare.

The nurse was relieved when the heart tests returned negative, so I felt better.

I told her, "Kevin has run five marathons. He has a strong heart."

She reminded me it wasn't unusual to have bad days, but he had been so good all of Thursday and Friday morning. I knew he would never be released to a rehabilitation center in this condition.

Although I prayed constantly, I couldn't stop crying. I was afraid I was losing Kevin after coming so far. I tried to lay my problems in the hands of God and allow myself to be a part of His plan no matter what it was. In my heart, I was afraid He planned to take Kevin's mind.

1 John 5
14 Now this is the confidence that we have in Him, that if we ask anything according to His will, He hears us. 15 And if we know that He hears us, whatever we ask, we know that we have the petitions that we have asked of Him.
(NKJV)

As the doctors and nurses came and went, I tried once more to read the Bible and prayed the storm would pass, leaving Kevin unharmed. I don't recall the book or chapter. The Bible was hard to understand. Reading helped me focus my prayers and left me feeling a little less stressed. I longed for the peace I felt when I gave the extubating over to God.

The second blood test on the heart attack was negative though he remained in and out of AFIB. The chest X-ray showed fewer dark spots on his lungs, but the EEG tracing his brain functions would run for another twenty-four hours.

He couldn't stick out his tongue or follow orders by early afternoon. I couldn't give him ice because I wasn't sure he could swallow or that he even understood what I was asking. He hadn't asked for any ice, and I knew he was thirsty. I feared he had given up.

I lowered the bar on the side of his bed and laid my head on his right shoulder. I shared music from my iPhone as I tried to get through to him. When the Kansas song, *Hold On* played, we both cried. I don't know if the song is about having faith in something outside us, but that's how I heard it that day.

> Where do you run when it's too much to bear
> Who do you turn to in need
> When nobody's there
> Outside your door he is waiting
> Waiting for you
> Sooner or later you know
> He's got to get through
> No hesitation and no holding back
> Let it all go and you'll know
> You're on the right track
> Hold on, baby, hold on
> 'Cause it's closer than you think
> And you're standing on the brink
> Hold on, baby, hold on
> 'Cause there's something on the way
> Your tomorrow's not the same as today

I had hoped his tears meant he understood what was being said to him, that there was still a piece of Kevin inside.

Leaving that night, I wasn't sure I would see him the next day. If I did, I didn't know if he would still know me.

On the way home, there was a beautiful sunset. I stopped to take a picture of it and took the time to thank God for all his gifts, most

especially the extra days I had with Kevin. That
had been my prayer the day I brought him in. I
had asked for a chance to say goodbye to Kevin,
and my prayer had been answered. I couldn't ask
for anything more.

ॐ📖ॐ

During Sunday morning rounds, the doctor
reminded me again of Kevin's Living Will
and DNR clause. I was overriding it each day and
kept Kevin on the feeding tube.

He was holding at 93% oxygen on the
smaller cannula until about 9:00 am when the
nurse had to bump it up to 9 liters. Over the past
few days, he had to go back on the forced heated
air in the morning, so it wasn't surprising that they
had to bump it up.

The EEG wasn't showing signs of seizures.
The tech said his readings were normal, but they
wanted to keep him on it another day. When I
looked at the readings with the pen jumping all
over so erratically, I tended to think the worst. It
would have been easier if the recording machine
were in another room.

Around 11:00 am, one of the counselors
came in to reevaluate the plan to move Kevin into
a rehabilitation center. Obviously, the move
needed to be rescheduled. The counselor also
asked me about Kevin's DNR clause. I knew
Kevin would absolutely hate being tied to a

wheelchair and unable to eat. He loved cooking and has always been active, running, hiking, and swimming. Was I wrong to keep trying? While I was prepared to take care of him no matter what, I wasn't sure that was what he would want. What kind of life would that be?

The night nurse had said he was in and out of AFIB all night, but the outs were getting longer. By 1:00 pm, he was stable but still on the Amiodarone drip. The new chest X-rays were about the same, and all the blood gases were good.

Occasionally, Kevin woke for moments that morning, and he was very disoriented. I could tell he didn't know me when he opened his eyes. He couldn't tell us his name or where he was. Kevin could no longer answer yes or no questions, stick out his tongue or form any words. That he could wiggle his toes and fingers when asked was a sign that he might not have lost his motor skills. One miracle at a time. I was good with that.

By noon he was back down to 5 liters of oxygen, running at 97%, and down to 4 liters of oxygen by 3 pm. His heart rate had been steady.

That afternoon, Kevin had three lucid awakenings for about a minute each. He nodded yes when I asked him if he knew who I was, but he didn't know my name. I have renewed empathy for those who have family members with Alzheimer's. It is heartrending to lose someone while they are still alive.

Kerry and Erowyn left for New Hampshire this afternoon. I was grateful she didn't have to see her dad like this. Guy has been a rock. I could tell he was worried, but he always had a smile for me when we traded off.

The neurologist had scheduled an MRI at 3:00. Unfortunately, the emergency room was overrun, so the MRI was pushed back to 8:00 pm. We won't have results until morning. If it's brain damage from strokes, he may or may not recover some functions.

Seeing him so lost and alone was frightening. He couldn't tell us what was wrong or if he was hurting because he couldn't talk. I was genuinely afraid I'd gone too far. His body seemed to be recovering, but his mind was completely gone.

All the way home, I prayed that this would be a temporary setback and that God would bring Kevin back to us healthy and whole. Each night I got on my knees and thanked God for my time with Kevin.

❧📖❧

On Monday morning, Kevin was down to two liters on the cannula, and his oxygen was in the 90s. Medication held his heart rate and blood pressure steady. He still struggled to speak but had a few lucid moments. Thankfully, he slept most of the time. His body needed healing. When he was awake, he was disoriented and frightened. Even in his sleep, he was swinging his right arm up to his shoulder hour after hour. I tried to get him to relax, but he wasn't even aware he was doing it. I tried holding it down briefly, but he got agitated. He didn't recognize me. I'm not sure he understood what was happening to him.

I wanted to help him, but I needed to let go of what I couldn't control. There was nothing I could do but show him that I loved him. I held his hand and rubbed his feet and legs. I played music and read to him.

I tried reading more of the Old Testament. I remember wishing Kevin was awake so he could explain it to me. I didn't recognize any of the stories or verses. I knew, in my heart, that help was in this book, but I didn't know how to find it. I prayed that God would give me the strength to be there for Kevin.

Psalm 119
My soul melts from heaviness; strengthen me according to your word.
[NKJV]

Down the hall, a family was crying and worried about their mother. The two boys must have been in their late teens, possibly with a mental disability. Their mother must have "coded" by the sounds of their anguish. They were begging her to open her eyes and come back to them. Hearing their cries tore my soul to pieces, and I was once more overwhelmed with guilt. Was it selfish for me to want Kevin to be whole again?

"Lord, give me strength to navigate this storm, and please, help this family. They need You, too."

Guy came in so I could get something to eat. I went to the cafeteria, but I was too anxious to eat. I bought a salad and brought it to the room.

There was no change in Kevin when I got back. He was still swinging his arm, and he was talking nonstop gibberish. He didn't seem to know anyone was in the room. The doctor said the MRI showed a cluster of several dozen mini-strokes. Some of the scars were from older strokes. Apparently, when I thought he was having a seizure, he was having a stroke. How many times can one's heart break?

Like every night the past few days, leaving him was hard. I didn't know what tomorrow would bring, but I prayed for the best. I told him how much I loved him and said goodbye.

The night was agonizing, and I didn't sleep for more than an hour. My prayers were confused. As much as I wanted Kevin to regain his health, I kept thinking about the family down the hall. It felt so selfish to ask for Kevin's life.

෯📖෯

Kevin was asleep when I arrived on Tuesday morning, but all his numbers looked good. He woke up around 7:00 am and said, "I love you." This was the sign I needed. Kevin was still in there and lucid for nearly an hour. Throughout the morning, he drifted away several times but only for about 30 seconds and once for about a half hour. I didn't know if these zoning-out moments were more strokes, his medication, or sheer exhaustion.

He said several complete sentences, but the words were still hard to understand. At least now, the words were in the correct order when I could understand them.

For obvious reasons, he couldn't eat or drink. I spoke with the doctor about a gastral tube, but he assured me it was too soon to think about that. His Echocardiogram came back good, and he pooped three times. I know it sounds silly, but it is an essential function. This meant his body was recovering. Unfortunately, he can't exercise with all the wires attached to his head.

When he wasn't zoned out, he talked up a storm. His speech was garbled, but I almost understood what he was saying. Anyone who knows Kevin knows the guy can talk.

I tried to keep him awake during the day because the nurse said he was awake most of the night. I believe he slept during the day because he knew I was there with him, keeping him safe. He never was one to be alone.

That afternoon, he was moved to a stroke/cardiac unit room. His left side was still weak compared to the right side, and the feeling in his skin from side to side was slightly different. He has always had an irregular heartbeat, triggering the monitors' alarms and freaking me out. I worried he was having another stroke and losing ground every time he zoned out. The damage from the cluster of mini strokes set him back at least a week if not two.

All hope of having him home by mid-July was dashed. He would never come home if he couldn't recover his mental acuity. During his neural test, he looked at pictures but couldn't tell us what he saw. He was good at repeating words but stumbled when asked a question. If the therapy worked, we would see gradual changes over the next few days.

When I got home that night, I updated Kevin's Facebook page and thanked our friends and family for their support. It was hard to believe it was still June. I felt like I'd been on a six-month safari in the wild jungles of Africa.

I got a notice on Facebook that a close friend had passed the night before. I felt agony for his wife. It was so sudden. I couldn't help but feel guilty that I still had Kevin. I had been given the days to say goodbye and make peace with losing him. I sincerely thanked God. I prayed for a full recovery because I knew God could do anything. I also prayed that God would be with all my dear friends who lost loved ones. I asked him to watch over all the nurses and doctors and guide these precious caregivers in their work.

❧ 📖 ❦

Wednesday was another tough day. I tried to read the bible to Kevin, but he couldn't concentrate. He was obsessed with his phone, but we couldn't get into it because I got locked out by trying too many passwords. He kept rambling on about the Libertarian Party and who was a good Christian or good Libertarian. Trying to understand him was challenging. The sentences didn't make sense; some were incomplete, and others seemed to be totally different topics. I tried to change the subject but couldn't get through to him. He was repeating the same thing over and over again. He looked so stressed and so frustrated; it was heartbreaking to watch.

Surprisingly, Kevin had a lucid spell when the speech therapist stopped by. He gave clear and concise answers to almost everything. He wasn't ready to have the feeding tube removed, but it was an improvement over the morning. I got my hopes up, thinking we were past the worst.

Unfortunately, he got sluggish in the afternoon and began slurring his words. I think he was focusing on a bible story. He kept repeating the same things. He talked about God making him choose who was good and who was paying for sins. He prattled on about a woman giving birth to twin monkeys. Kevin was unconscious during these ramblings and wouldn't wake. He moved a lot, bending both legs and lifting them off the bed, similar to his neuromotor function tests.

By the time I had to leave, he was doing math problems out loud. He seemed less stressed doing the math, but he was talking to someone in another dimension. I prayed this was his damaged brain recreating pathways to the things locked in his head.

He didn't know I was in the room or when I left for the night. I was still praying for a full recovery. I knew God had the power; I needed to have the faith.

☙📖❧

I couldn't believe it was already the first of July. Kevin had bounced back from the ventilator so quickly that first week that I honestly thought he would be home by mid-July. Seeing him in this lost state was hard, but I didn't give up— something so unlike me. Seeing anything through to the finish has never been my strong suit.

The night nurse said Kevin slept through the night. They couldn't wake enough to do more than squeeze hands and wiggle toes during the night checks. I didn't know if that was good or bad.

They let him sleep until 8:30 before the nurse did a neuro assessment. He passed it with flying colors. He held both arms up for a count of ten and both legs for a count of five. He could give his name and birthday and tell us he was at Adventist Hospital in Parker. Most impressive was that he said he was in the hospital because of a heart attack. He was a completely different person than the man I had left the night before. Kevin was back.

Unfortunately, ten minutes later, when the doctor asked, he said he was in the hospital because he had rolled the jeep. While the doctor was in the room, Kevin zoned out for a short time. I still didn't know if these lapses were mini-strokes. The doctor never confirmed or dismissed the possibility of strokes.

Whatever the prognosis, Kevin would have a tough time regaining his finer motor skills. The dexterity in his left hand would likely never return.

Our friends, Matt and Nick, came to see him in the morning. He was happy to see them and reasonably lucid while they were in the room. He also had a FaceTime call with Kelly and Gay.

By noon he was showing signs of confusion again and having trouble speaking. He didn't take any calls in the afternoon, and Victoria only stayed for about an hour.

After they left, I tried to get Kevin to relax, but he had some large muscle twitches like yesterday. Mostly his right arm was constantly reaching up to his head. That constant movement was bound to leave his arm sore. I was hoping his brain was rewiring his muscles because he was still imitating the neuro tests, lifting his legs, and squeezing his hands in his sleep.

I thought he might have been overwhelmed with all the activity, so I decided to limit the visitors to two hours for Guy and half an hour for one other person for the next few days to see if I could keep him from zoning out in the afternoons. He wouldn't sleep if anyone were in the room other than me, and he needed sleep to heal.

It took me 30 minutes to get him to sleep that afternoon, and the nurse came in 10 minutes later. That happened three times. By the end of the day, Kevin was so agitated that his heart started racing, and respiration went way up.

The doctor said he was suffering from a form of ICU Delirium. Common symptoms include disorientation, inability to sustain attention, impaired short-term memory, impaired visuospatial ability, reduced level of consciousness, and perseveration. Common behavioral symptoms include sleep-wake cycle disturbance, irritability, hallucinations, and delusions.

The nurse gave him something for delirium that should calm him. I was hoping for another ice cube or two for him. He was thirsty and hungry, but we didn't see any therapists. He looked upset when I had to leave.

On the drive home the last few days, I started noticing flowers, trees, and sunsets. Everything was so much more vivid. I found myself thanking God that it was summertime and that I didn't have to drive back and forth in the snow. I found myself thinking about God more each day. Yes, most of it was praying for Kevin, but over the weeks, I realized how truly incredible the universe is.

At home, I said my prayers and updated our Facebook friends. I thanked them for their prayers and the love they continued to send. Reading their comments every night gave me so much hope. I had never felt so loved. The Lord God truly works miracles.

❧📖❧

Friday began like every other day. I have a new appreciation of what so many other people have been through. This wasn't any fun at all. Kevin was very agitated all morning. He had a fitful night of sleep, and I couldn't seem to calm him for more than a minute. It scared me so.

He almost pulled himself into a sitting position, so I thought he might be ready to sit in a wheelchair. I hoped his regular therapists would see this and let him go somewhere in a chair. He needed to get out of his room. Any change would ease his agitation and confusion.

The physical therapist came in, but she didn't have a partner, so he didn't get to sit on the side of the bed, much less go for a ride. He did all the exercises and then hyperventilated, so I tried to get him to rest.

I got him to sleep, but he only dozed for about thirty seconds. I was at a loss for what to do. It doesn't help when someone comes to take his vitals or asks him what his name is every hour. I thought Kevin needed REM sleep. I wanted the therapists and doctors to see him. Still, I wish the nurses didn't have to turn him from side to side every two hours, on top of having his blood drawn, neural tests, feeding tube changes, and medication replacements.

His doctor stopped by in the afternoon. The good news was that they thought his heart and lungs were stable enough to go to a rehabilitation facility. The bad news was that he still couldn't swallow and might need a gastral tube. If they place a gastral tube, it would be for a minimum of three months, and there can be compilations with infections and reactions. That meant no solid food or drink.

The doctor gave us until Monday to let them know what we wanted to do. He needed to pass a barium test before they would take out the nose feeder. Unfortunately, he was in that "not all here" place he struggled with on Wednesday.

His mouth was so dry he was begging for ice. Even one or two cubes would have been so wonderful. At the same time, I was afraid that if the speech therapist saw him like this, she wouldn't even try the ice, and he would be condemned to a gastral tube. I was so afraid I'd made a mistake overriding his DNR. I prayed once more.

"Please, God, let him pass the swallow test. I can deal with the twitches and feeding him, but please let him enjoy food. Please calm his shattered mind so he may rest and heal. In Jesus' name, Amen."

At about noon, the doctor came in to check Kevin's stools. There was blood in it, so they stopped the blood thinner he was on and scheduled a Colonoscopy and upper track procedure for Sunday. Kevin eats Tums like candy. I was betting he had an ulcer, and the Eliquis caused it to bleed. By evening, they had given him two pints of blood.

The speech therapist came in but said Kevin had too much mucus in the back of the throat to do a swallow test, so no ice.

She gave me something to spritz in his mouth every hour to break down the mucus. His mouth was so dry. I sprayed the Bio Mist in his mouth every half hour and sucked out any mucus I could find, but he really hated it. Hopefully, his throat will be clear enough for ice tomorrow.

Kevin was lucid most of the afternoon but still couldn't talk. Some of that was due to the mucus clogging his mouth and throat.

When the nurse did the neural test that evening, he got twelve wrong. A twelve means he failed twelve questions out of thirty. The average for a man his age is four. He was at ten on Thursday and as much as twenty on the first day they tested for stroke effects. The exam consists of having him hold up his arms and legs and asking if he can tell the difference between touches. Of course, they asked his name, date of birth, current month and year, etc. They had him read words and sentences. Lastly, they showed him a drawing and asked what was happening in the picture.

After the nurse left, he was super agitated. His hands were strapped into big mitts because he had no control over the swinging of his right arm. To ensure he wouldn't tear out any of his wires, he had to wear these unless I was holding his hand or they were taking blood.

[121]

By this time, he knew where he was and didn't like it at all. I tried to explain why he needed to stay in the hospital, but he kept begging me to take him home. There was nothing I would have liked better than to have him home. It was so hard to deny him.

Before I left, I told the nurse to watch him because he was almost strong enough to get out of bed by himself, and I was afraid he would hurt himself.

I thanked God for his truly wonderful family and friends. They were my support group. Kevin and I had been on this roller coaster for nearly three weeks, and I wasn't sure he was any closer to coming home.

❧📖❧

Kevin seemed slightly less disoriented when I arrived on Saturday morning. He was less angry, and his speech was clearer. This was probably due to getting more rest and removing much of the mucus in his throat.

He had pulled out his feeding tube during the night, and they had to replace it. I had put the mitt back on before I left last night, but he pulled it off with his teeth.

He still wasn't sleeping for extended times, but it was deeper sleep. He would usually doze for about five to ten minutes each time.

His GI tract bleeding continued, and his kidneys showed a blip in function. This warranted another ultrasound. Thankfully, the ultrasound came back normal.

Kevin got a six on his neural test today. That was a significant improvement. Part of the test is to repeat a word the nurse says. His pronunciation was good until the nurse said, "Huckleberry."

Kevin said, "Hound."

The nurse was young, and she repeated the word Huckleberry to Kevin. Again, he said, "Hound."

She looked at me confused, and I told her Huckleberry Hound was an old cartoon character. We had a good laugh.

He was still stumbling on the year but did better on other things. He could read, although he stumbled over some words. That he could read at all was fabulous. The involuntary ticks stopped as well. He looked so much more at peace. The doctor said he just needed to find or make new pathways to the memories. I was ecstatic over his improvement because he didn't even know who I was two days ago.

The best news was that his throat was clear enough to have a popsicle! His being able to eat had been an enormous worry. Kevin loves food. I prayed we could take out the feeding tube now.

For dinner, he ate ground chicken with gravy, peaches, 7up, and vanilla pudding. His dinner was followed by something to clean his colon. That was unpleasant.

I didn't realize how exhausted I was until I got home. I know God was carrying me because I could not have done this alone.

While updating everyone on Kevin's progress that night, I saw a meme on Facebook. It profoundly touched me, so I made it my screen saver.

"I will lead you to the river so you can remember how beautiful it feels to be moved by something that is out of your control" – Emery Allen

When I lived in Nevada, several friends and I went rafting down the Colorado River. The river was deep and swift. Our small rafts and inner tubes were no match for the force of the water. It was marvelously relaxing.

Remembering this feeling, I let go of the worry and truly rested. I allowed God to take control of my life's river.

☙📖❧

On Sunday morning, Kevin was sleeping when I got there. The nurse said he had been coherent when they woke him for vitals. When we talked, Kevin was calm, and his speech was better. He scored a six again on his morning neural test. Different things drifted, but overall, it was about the same as Saturday.

He wasn't allowed food on Sunday because of the colonoscopy scheduled for 8:00 am. The stuff they gave him overnight to clean his colon may have irritated whatever was going on inside, causing him to bleed again. They gave him more blood, and he seemed to tolerate it well.

They had to postpone the colonoscopy because his potassium was too low. They rescheduled the procedure and started replacing his potassium. It was a shame because he was looking forward to eating lunch.

He desperately wanted to get out of the hospital, but I couldn't take him home until he could sit up alone and walk to the toilet.

I told him, "If the colonoscopy goes well, we could look at a rehabilitation center by Wednesday, July 7th. Then it should only be two or three more weeks."

At roughly 3:00, they removed the nasal feeding tube for his colonoscopy and upper GI scope. His doctor said we could see how he does on solid food. That was so encouraging. I prayed the bleeding problem would be easy to fix.

I tried reading the Bible while I waited for the procedure to be completed. I am absolutely convinced God had been carrying me through the past three weeks. I still couldn't understand the most straightforward verses. I settled for reading prayers from Kevin's family.

It was 5:00 pm before they brought Kevin back to his room. I had hoped he wouldn't be too tired to eat, but he was exhausted when he got his food. He ate a few bites, but not enough to replace the nasal feeding tube nutrients.

I was afraid we would be looking at a gastral tube if he didn't finish his breakfast in the morning. I asked if he could do protein shakes, and the doctor said we would take it a day at a time.

When I get upset and worried, I realize it's because I'm trying to control things that are out of my hands. Turning things over to God sounds easy, but it isn't. I constantly fell back into trying to control Kevin's progress. This challenge showed me how much I could hand over to God.

When the control bug started biting at my heels, I chose to thank God for the time we had together, and as the worry slid to the back of my mind, I rested in God's peace.

It was still light when I had to leave for the day. I opened his shade and turned his bed toward the window so he could watch for fireworks. He was sad that I couldn't stay and watch with him. Honestly, I was so tired I went straight to bed and didn't see a single firework show.

I have included a copy of Kelly's July 4th post because it is a vivid example of the daily miracles that proved God was watching over us.

Kelly's Post July 4
"What an absolute roller coaster the past 3 weeks have been. On Monday, as we drove to CT, I learned that dad's MRI revealed that he had several mini-strokes. For those who have been reading these updates, you could probably sense how disheartening this news was. But literally, moments after I shared that update, we pulled up behind this truck & it had the message **"God is moving. Be patient"** on it. We stayed near it all the way to our stop to stay over for the evening & for some reason, it just helped me refocus my energy.
We know all too well that lows will come with the highs, so we're asking for prayer that dad's colonoscopy and upper GI scope come back clear & reveal that whatever is causing the blood in his stool is easily treatable & not overly concerning. We pray for continued cognitive improvement & physical strength & that his next chest X-ray shows tremendous improvement in the opacities caused by COVID.

God IS moving…we are so grateful. Still working on the patience."

≈📖≈

Monday morning, Kevin was awake when I got to the hospital. He was very coherent but still slurs a bit. It takes a lot of energy to talk. He was uncomfortable, but I couldn't zero in on where he hurt, somewhere in his chest. He had another EKG for chest pains. I think this made number five or six.

His left arm with his PIC line was cold and swollen. We were still waiting for the ultrasound on the arm. I thought the vein might be leaking. I have had experience with that, and I felt like his nurse had never seen it before. She tried to tell me it was because he wasn't moving. Fluid leaking from the PIC line could be dangerous, but I trusted her knowledge.

He ate over half of his breakfast and ate all his lunch. Surprisingly, he watched tv most of the day. He hadn't wanted it on until today. I took that as another good sign that he was coming back to us.

He was still losing blood, so at 1:30, they took him to get a CT scan of his small intestines to look for the bleeding. He had to have four more liters of blood.

He was gone over three hours, and the tech who wheeled him out said it would be forty minutes. Guy and I were hoping that meant they were fixing whatever was wrong. It's hard not to worry when you don't know what is happening.

As it turned out, the anesthesiologist couldn't find a vein, so they were going to postpone the procedure. While preparing Kevin to return to his room, a nurse asked the anesthesiologist if he had tried the PIC line. Well, he hadn't, and the rest, they say, is history. They went ahead and completed the procedure, albeit a little later.

Kevin was exhausted from the three-hour trip to radiology. He didn't eat dinner until 7:30 pm. He could feed himself a little until they put a new IV in his good arm to give him more blood.

I stayed until 9:00 pm to feed him the rest of his dinner. It was hard to leave when he was awake and wanting to talk. Visiting hours were over at 8:00 pm, but the nurse was fine with me feeding him.

I hadn't wanted to take a picture of him in the hospital. For the most part, I didn't think I wanted to remember how terrible he looked during the past three weeks. In writing this book, I realize how important these memories are. With each day I recount, I renew my faith in God.

I am so grateful to God for the gifts he has given me. I was so sure I would lose Kevin when he couldn't talk anymore. I prayed with all my heart every day and every night.

By July 5th, it was almost as if the strokes had never happened. I know many people who have suffered more significant losses than I have, and I pray they will find peace in God's love. I am in awe of God. I wish I had turned to him earlier in my life.

❧📖❧

Kevin was awake when I came in on Tuesday morning, July 6th. He started watching the clock at about 5:00 am. I was walking on air because Kevin had come so far in only two days. He was considerably weaker than the day when they removed the ventilator, but Kevin was a hard worker. I had no doubt he would recover his strength in time.

He ate all his breakfast but was in pain by lunch, so he only nibbled at his food.

His Gastral Internist said they didn't find anything in the upper track. The lower track had a couple of older blood clots, but she couldn't tell where the blood was coming from. There is a way to X-ray the smaller intestines, but the dye could jack with his kidneys. Since his kidneys weren't fully recovered, they decided to give it a day to see if the bleeding would stop. There was a possibility that when he went back on the blood thinner, he would start bleeding again, and we would have to do the dye test.

He complained of chest pains, but an EKG didn't show anything wrong with his heart. A while later, they took him down for a CT of his lungs.

Our friend Beatriz came by shortly after he came back from the CT procedure. Kevin was confused and in even more pain. I don't think he knew what was happening.

The CT scan showed he had pneumonia and wasn't getting enough oxygen to his lower left lung, which likely was causing the pain. The nurse bumped his oxygen back up to eleven liters, the maximum outside of the ICU. Ten minutes later, they transferred him back to the ICU.

⇜📖⇝

By a miracle of God, Kevin survived a cardiac arrest, six days on a ventilator, and several dozen mini-strokes. Each time, he had recovered all his senses quickly. Only to be bounced back to the ICU with pneumonia the following week. In just over three weeks, his life was once more hanging by a thread.

I can't describe how scary this was. Every time Kevin was about to be released, he was knocked back to square one. I felt like I was rolling a boulder uphill, only to have it roll back over me again and again.

In the ICU, Kevin was put on a BIPAP, a giant breathing machine with a full facemask. The forced air was awful, and Kevin fought it with every ounce of his weakened strength. They strapped him down to the bed like a crazy person. He was terrified, and it didn't help that I was frightened for him.

The doctors told me they would have to put him back on the ventilator if they couldn't control his breathing within the next hour. I spoke with Kevin, and he said he would be reintubated if necessary. I was uncertain because the success rate of reintubation was marginal. He had to be sedated again because he tried to tear off the BIPAP mask. I had never seen him so frightened.

I prayed the steroids would address the pneumonia and work quickly. The following 24 hours were critical.

Leaving him was more challenging than any other night, and so many had been challenging. Every night as I left the hospital, I prayed. I was so thankful for my time with this man and that he led me back to Jesus.

On the way home from the hospital, my prayers changed. This was the first night I didn't pray for Kevin's healing. I now understand that God has a plan, which might not be what I want. I prayed that if God needed to take Kevin, please make it quick. *"Please, Lord, don't make him suffer through the pain and fear. I am ready to accept your plan because I know it is best for me. I am ready to let Kevin go. I know I'm going to be okay."* I kept repeating to myself, *"Let go and let God."* By the time I pulled into the driveway, I was at peace. I had given Kevin to God.

While Jesus was in the garden of Gethsemane, he prayed, *"Father, if you are willing, take this cup from me; yet not my will, but yours be done."* Luke 22: 42 (NIV)

At the time, I was unaware of this Bible verse. When I read it months later, I was certain the holy spirit had been guiding my thoughts and teaching me how to find peace in God's will.

I opened my Facebook app, intending to write an update, and I was once again overwhelmed by the outpouring of love. I felt truly blessed to know that so many people loved, cared for, and were praying for Kevin. I was beyond humbled by the love we had been shown. In reading the comments, I had another epiphany.

This was God's love surrounding me. It was so thick that it was a physical feeling. I dropped to my knees at the side of the bed and thanked God for loving me. I prayed that God would bless everyone who had been so attentive to our needs.

I dropped off to sleep feeling safe and warm for the first time in weeks.

❧📖❧

The next few days are fuzzy. I remember lots of medication running into Kevin's arms, and he was so discouraged. The last time he was in the ICU, we celebrated every intravenous medication that was removed. Now, all the lines were back, and it felt like we were starting over again.

The ultrasound for the unexplained issue with the PICC line in his arm showed a small clot. I didn't know if that was good news or not.

We discussed the stomach gastral tube again. On the plus side, the internal bleeding appeared to have stopped, so the doctor restarted the blood thinners. These drugs are essential to prevent strokes. So far, it doesn't appear Kevin has lost much of his motor skills.

The BIPAP machine seemed to be working. He was able to have it off long enough to eat his meals. He had a fever, so they gave him antibiotics and something to open the airways.

It was just one thing after another. I knew that God was in control, and when I couldn't think of the words to pray, I just repeated, *"I trust You, Lord, I trust You, Lord, I trust You, Lord. Thank You, Lord, for this day. You have been so good to us."*

Thursday morning, he was anxious, scared, and frustrated. I believe this was shaking his faith, and that truly frightened him. Kevin grew up in the church and was always a true believer in Jesus Christ. This trial was a genuine test of his faith. While mine grew stronger every day, his faith seemed to waver.

The doctor came in around 7:00 am to let me know Kevin was on the border of returning to the ventilator. Going back on the ventilator meant learning to swallow again, which may or may not happen. The ventilator does terrible things to the throat. We would be looking at ninety weeks of recovery, and it would be unlikely he could do something like cooking, sailing, and hiking. If he had to be on the ventilator longer than five days, he probably wouldn't recover the use of his body. He would require tracheotomy and full-time nursing care. I knew he wouldn't want that, but he said he would try the ventilator if necessary. I had this same conversation with his doctor and his family only two weeks earlier. The steroids would take a couple of days, so we didn't expect a significant change that day.

Character is formed in difficulty, but I was getting weary of the battle. Prayer was the only thing in my toolbox, the only thing I could control. I had given Kevin over to God and his will. While Kevin slept, I prayed that the steroids would work quickly. At the same time, I was thankful for another day with him. I was grateful for the love of his amazing family.

His oxygen needs were lower when he was sleeping, and his respiration dropped into the twenties, where it should be. Unfortunately, he couldn't eat if he was asleep.

When I tried to feed him that morning, he had trouble swallowing water, so I didn't dare give him any solid food. He only had about one egg, three Ensures, and three fruit cups all day yesterday. I hated to wake him for another swallow test, but if he couldn't eat solid food, we needed to reinsert the nasal feeder. Thankfully, he was able to eat a small amount.

Kevin was taken off the BIPAP breathing machine around 9:00 am. During rounds, Doctor Waas was slightly less concerned about moving Kevin to the ventilator. Kevin was awake and breathing on his own for an hour before needing the BIPAP machine again. That didn't mean it couldn't still be required, but the odds of not reintubating Kevin were a little better. Doctor Wass quoted me 50/50 odds at 7:00 am, and now, at 10:00 am, it looked more like 60/40.

❧📖❧

My sister, Bette, called to tell me she had set up a Go Fund Me Page to help with Kevin's medical bills. Like my mom, my first reaction was, "Absolutely Not! I can do this without anyone's help." Asking for help was embarrassing. Just having friends mow my lawn was humbling enough. I couldn't ask our friends for money.

The bills were increasing daily, and I felt like I had almost reached rock bottom. This would take all our retirement savings, and I might need to sell the car, the camper, and the jeep.

Over the last four weeks, my priorities changed. Anyone who knows me knows how much I love my house. I enjoy throwing fundraising parties and entertaining. My house symbolized who I was in this world, but I no longer cared about it. I was happy to sell everything I owned to pay the medical bills. I would be content in a shoebox if I still had Kevin.

Bette asked me to think about the Go Fund Me Page.

When Kevin woke up, I asked him how he felt about charity. To my surprise, he was okay with the page. He didn't want to lose the house.

I told Kevin, "I already told God the house was His if that's what it takes to have a few more days with you."

After talking with Kevin, I caved and told my sister to go ahead and launch the page. This was a massive change for me. I had always been fiercely independent. Not being able to get into our banking accounts was nothing compared to asking people for money to pay our bills. We went to a convention without taking precautions. We were responsible for getting sick. We owed this bill.

In the afternoon, Kevin met with Doctor Johnson, the heart/respiratory specialist. Emergency medical technicians often break ribs during CPR. She was looking for a possible fracture, punctured lung, or other things that might be causing Kevin's painful breathing. She ordered a skeletal X-ray for the morning. Doctor Johnson also ordered an anti-anxiety medication that made Kevin a little fuzzy but helped with his breathing.

Kevin said, "Being stoned isn't all that bad."

After his physical therapy, they had to bump Kevin up to the high-pressure oxygen. He didn't get to sit, but he got some stretching.

I watched the therapists so I could do his stretches and exercises when a therapist couldn't come in. There were only four physical and two speech therapists for the entire hospital. There were many days their caseloads were too heavy to see Kevin.

Kevin got a sponge bath from his nurse Larissa, who was fantastic. He felt better after the bath and could still keep his breathing under forty. His breathing was still too rapid. When he hyperventilates, his breath doesn't stay in his lungs long enough to extract the oxygen. His breathing should be under twenty, but if he stayed under sixty, he wouldn't have to wear the IPAP mask.

Kerry sent me a link to a yoga teacher. Unfortunately, he couldn't concentrate on the video. However, he fell asleep, which was good for him.

He had no appetite for dinner but managed the protein shakes, peaches, and a popsicle. I often felt like I was pushing him too hard, but I couldn't stop. It was like a force outside me was driving me to be with him every day, feeding him and exercising his arms and legs.

He scored a six and a seven on his neural test during the shift change. Most of the points he lost were from being so tired. He could no longer hold up his legs and arms. He was losing more muscle mass every day. However, he was spot on answering cognitive questions, a significant improvement from a few days ago when he couldn't remember his name.

He was alert, so I stayed until 8:30 pm. I prayed on the way home, as I always did during those days. I was calm and felt an unusual sense of serenity that I can't, to this day, explain. It was as if by telling God I was okay with losing Kevin, all my worries and anxieties were erased. It was out of my control, and I was okay with that for the first time in my life.

When I got home, I found a note from Payton. Kevin was introduced to Payton by his daughter, Kerry, many years ago, and they have stayed in touch. He is now a dear friend of mine, one of many I met through Kevin's fight with COVID.

From Payton
"In the darkest hour... I am with you. In the lowest valley... I am with you. You will meet with me on the highest mountain top. A mountain top in the heavens when your labor is completed, but not until your labor is finished. Michele, when you only see one set of footprints in the sand, it is Jesus's footprints, and he is carrying us."

❧📖❦

Friday morning, Kevin was sleeping peacefully when I arrived. He was still on high-pressure oxygen at thirty liters but, thankfully, no IPAP or ventilator. That was a long way from where he needed to be to move out of the ICU, but it was an improvement from last night.

A couple of different doctors came to see him. They did another Echocardiogram. Another X-ray showed a build-up of what might be fluid in his lungs but was most likely Organizing Pneumonia, something they see in COVID lungs. It's treatable with steroids but might not be totally reversible.

Kevin still had no appetite but ate because I made him eat.

Kevin's sister, Gay, and Dwayne arrived around 3:00 pm. It was good to see them. They are so warm and loving. It's the kind of love I see in real Christians, like my brother and his wife, Cheri. It's the kind of genuine love I have come to really appreciate.

At home, Gay and Dwayne helped put my prayers into words. I praised God for pulling Kevin through so many tough days and thanked Him for all the extra time I had with Kevin. I had been given the time to make peace with what the future holds and no longer felt like I needed to control it.

Over the past two days, Kevin had been asking me something I couldn't understand. It frustrated both of us. While Gay was visiting on Saturday, she figured it out. Kevin wanted to hear some music by George Beverly Shea, a gospel singer I had never heard. Gay played a few songs on her phone and sang hymns with Kevin.

This was the music they grew up with. When Kevin was young, his sister and brothers formed a small gospel group that entertained at retirement homes and performed at Central Baptist church. Two of his older brothers went into the ministry, and Gay works for a retirement home.

God works in astonishing ways. Of all the hospitals I could have driven to that Monday morning, I chose Adventist in Parker.

There were four or five different ministers and pastors on call and one of them stopped in every day to pray with us. Each day at 10:00 am, the hospital shared a prayer of healing over the intercom. The artwork depicting Jesus with health workers and biblical verses on paintings throughout the hospital was so comforting. I was humbled by the outpouring of love and prayers for us, not only from friends but from staff members.

The number of cards and letters Kevin received was delightful. Until now, he hadn't been able to read them at all. Watching him recognize how many people loved him brought me such joy.

So many of you will never realize how much you've done to keep us encouraged. The sweet comments and powerful prayers that took precious time to type up and send to us were life-giving. So often, they were perfectly timed, arriving when I struggled to put words together or felt my faith shaken.

I was not familiar with many stories in the Bible, but Kelly shared this with me. Moses had to hold his arms up when Israel was battling the Amalekites. Every time Moses would start to drop his arms, the Israelites would struggle, so Aaron and Hur stepped in and held up Moses's arms. They rolled a stone for Moses to sit on and held his arms up until the Israelites prevailed.

It is a blessing to have others lift our arms during this battle when we have been too tired, too scared, or too overwhelmed to do so ourselves.

As the days passed, I tried to set my worries aside and enjoy my time with Kevin.

"Heavenly Father, I thank you for these precious moments with Kevin. Please instill your peace in him so he can be free of the anxiety that is crushing his soul. Bless the many people who have sent love and prayers to us. Forgive me for my moments of doubt and fear. In Jesus' name, Amen."

☙📖❧

The following week was up and down. Kevin was in and out of AFIB, and while we had some scary respiratory moments, Kevin improved. We dodged the ventilator and the gastral Tube. The steroids improved his breathing.

Kevin had a couple of scary bouts with speaking. It wasn't like the aphasia he had before. It was more like he couldn't remember how to say the words. I was concerned he had suffered another stroke. As frustrating as it was, I prayed he would recover from this new trial.

He could almost feed himself with his right hand, and we continued working his legs daily. Unfortunately, we couldn't exercise his back and core until his breathing stabilized.

Kevin's bottom was starting to get sore but being propped up on his side hurt his chest. The nurses came in to change the side wedges every two hours. He begged me to take them out after about thirty minutes. Because he was showing signs of Footdrop, I put the wedges at the end of the bed to keep his foot from drifting to the side. This usually led me to exercise his feet, legs, and arms, which was beneficial.

He was still bleeding internally, but it slowed down drastically. Although he was holding steady on the smaller cannula, his respiration was too rapid.

One of my devotionals was about trusting Jesus, taking one day at a time, and looking for the lesson in my troubles. I thank God for finding me worthy of this trial, and I will do my best to honor Him with my actions.

I continued to pray that Kevin's breathing would slow into a relaxed and deep pattern, that his lungs would continue to heal, and that his kidneys would recover. Honestly, I am thankful God knew Kevin's many needs because I could never keep the list straight.

Kerry and Kelly took the time to call their dad almost every day. Family support was and is so essential for Kevin and for all those whose are sick. I hoped the powers-that-be learned through the COVID pandemic to stop isolating people. It truly broke my heart to think of all the people who were enduring this nightmare alone. My life would have been so completely different if it weren't for the love of Kevin's family. Praise to God and to all the medical professionals God orchestrated to give me this extra time with him. We have witnessed miracle after miracle over the past month.

Each night, I continued praying there would be no more setbacks. The setbacks were as hard emotionally as they were physically, maybe harder. I couldn't bear to see Kevin lose hope again. He was so thin and frail.

[144]

The complexity of the human body astounds me. The doctor told me most of the brain was personality. Motor skills only take up about ten percent of the brain, which is probably why I didn't recognize the earlier strokes. Most minor strokes change little things, like how someone likes their eggs or favorite ice cream flavor. I've seen some of these differences. When we first met, Kevin liked his eggs over easy. Now he claims he has always favored scrambled. How odd.

By Saturday, July 17th, the only IV he had running was potassium. Just a week ago, there were eight different lines of medication. I did a little happy dance every time they took another line away.

He was back on the smaller cannula and running between four and eight liters. The heated high-flow oxygen machine is standard in the ICU, so it was still beside the bed. I had hoped we had seen the last of that beast.

While he was waiting to go to surgery to have a filter put in his vein to catch any blood clots in the legs from reaching his heart, Kevin thumbed through his Bible. His shaking made it too hard to read, so he asked me to get him a large font bible with the words of Jesus printed in red.

I had no idea there were so many different Bible translations. I looked online but couldn't see the text inside the Bibles. I only had the description to go by. I ordered a Bible whose description said, "large font, words of Jesus in red." Unfortunately, those were the only words in the book.

I tried reading the Bible to him. It still made little sense to me, but I was slowly beginning to understand. Every saint has a past, and because of Jesus, every sinner has a future.

He was hungry when he got back to the room at 11:00 am. He ate all his lunch of meatloaf, mashed potatoes, and broccoli. He ate four Jell-O servings, a popsicle, and a chocolate mousse. He wanted more, but I was afraid he would overeat and get sick since he hadn't had more than liquids for the past five days. That night, he ate all his dinner as well. It was good to see his appetite return. The ups and downs were so fast.

The doctor said he should move out of the ICU in the next two days. That was fantastic news. I praised the Lord for his mercy and love. Another prayer was answered. I couldn't understand why God was so good to me.

It was easier to leave at night because Kevin was in far better spirits. He was still anxious to get out of the hospital, but he might have finally realized how dreadfully sick he was.

The following Sunday, we watched a "Church by the Glades" worship service on my laptop. If there is anything positive to come out of this pandemic, it's the ability to find numerous rich and excellent church services online.

The message that Sunday was about fear. The pastor was talking about how people ask for miracles all the time, but they don't want adversity. "God can't calm the waters if there is no storm." Covid is a storm that has affected us all in different ways. Looking around, you can see the abundant miracles the Lord has granted.

There is a storm raging, but I'm safe because Jesus is in the boat with me.

As the day wore on, we talked and laughed. It was like a rainbow after a storm. If there can be a perfect day in the hospital, this would be one. I ran across a story I want to share because it put all my trials into perspective.

There was once a group of women studying the book of Malachi in the Old Testament. As they were studying chapter three, they came across verse three: "He will sit as a refiner and purifier of silver." This verse puzzled the women, and they wondered what this statement meant about the character and nature of God. One of the women offered to find out about refining silver and get back to the group at their subsequent Bible study.

That week, the woman called a silversmith and made an appointment to watch him at work.

She didn't mention the reason for her interest beyond curiosity about the process. As she watched the silversmith, he held a piece of silver over the fire and let it heat up. He explained that in refining silver, one needed to keep the silver in the middle of the fire where the flames were hottest to burn away all the impurities.

The woman thought about God holding us in such a hot spot – then she thought again about the verse, that he sits as a refiner and purifier of silver. She asked the silversmith if it was true that he had to sit there in front of the fire the whole time the silver was being refined.

The man answered "Yes," and explained that he not only had to sit there holding the silver, but he had to keep his eyes on it the entire time it was in the fire. It would be damaged if the silver was left even a moment too long in the flame.

The woman was silent for a moment. Then she asked the silversmith, "How do you know when the silver is fully refined?"

He smiled at her and answered, "Oh, that's easy. When I see my image in it."

If today you are feeling the heat of this world's fire, just remember that God, our Father has His eyes on you.

I love this story; thanks, Anne Kephart, for sharing it! My heart is so full of love for the Lord; it feels like it could burst. By giving my worries over to Jesus, knowing he wouldn't leave me in the fire too long, I could enjoy the hours I had with Kevin as the gifts they were. Thank you, Lord.

&📖&

Day thirty-eight, and we were in the same place we were on day 8 of this journey. They moved Kevin into a regular room around 7:00 pm. I continued to pray that God would heal his brain and lungs, thankful Jesus was watching over us. I asked that his recovery would continue and that there would be no reason to return to the ICU. My heart couldn't take it again.

We met with a caseworker and doctor from a rehabilitation hospital the following day. Kevin wasn't strong enough for their program. He had lost too much muscle, so I searched for other options. I wanted to find a facility that wouldn't automatically require a fourteen-day isolation upon his arrival. Kevin doesn't do well alone. Since I had been with him every day for over a month, I hoped they would let me quarantine with him. A facility that allowed our dog, Bear, to visit would be excellent.

&📖&

On Monday, July 19th, Kevin's aphasia returned with a vengeance. He slipped in and out of coherent speech. He got so frustrated and angry. Kevin rarely gets angry, and it broke my heart to see him struggle with the most minor things. Although he was taking medication to help prevent stroke, he might have suffered more regardless. He was either repeating things over and over or couldn't form the words for what he wanted to say. I could see his frustration. His brain may have been rewiring itself, but it was hard to watch. He would have a few seconds of lucid speech and then go back to mumbling nonsense non-stop. He was so coherent on Sunday; he even remembered his phone password. I thought we were past the aphasia. This one was different. It was more frightening because it completely took over. One moment he was clear and sound; the next, he couldn't pronounce his name. He knew the answer but couldn't make his mouth say the words. He had several moments when he couldn't remember how to form a word. Oddly, he could spell them. Well, he didn't actually spell the word, but he could give us a couple of letters, and we could figure it out from there.

When the words did come out, he talked as if he had to say everything right now in case he could never speak again. There was such desperation in his eyes.

It felt like the moment we got a little bit ahead; something would slam into us, knocking the wind out of us again and again. Whenever

Kevin's physical body started to recover, it seemed his mental acuity would falter.

≈📖≈

By July 21st, I was utterly amazed at how far he had come after everything he had gone through. He was regularly eating now. They removed the PICC line. All the IV drip lines were off, and all his medications were oral. His lung capacity was slowly improving. The internal bleeding seemed to have stopped, though they never did figure out what had caused it.

Pneumonia was a considerable setback. Not only weakening Kevin's lungs, but he lost so much more muscle. At this stage, he couldn't even sit on the side of the bed without someone holding him. He couldn't raise his head off a pillow or turn over.

Doctor Johnson showed me Kevin's skeletal X-ray. The tip of his lower left rib was completely broken off. This explained the chest pain. There was nothing they could do at that point but let it continue to heal. Kevin felt vindicated by this news.

I found a nursing home willing to take Kevin. We had a long hard road ahead, but with love and prayers, we would come out better than before. This mountain taught me so much about empathy and letting go of things I can't control. The abundance of love I received made my connection to Jesus possible. God's love through others made my job easier.

I thank You, our great Creator, for the many gifts I have been given throughout my life. My blessings are too numerous to enumerate.

❧📖❦

The following week, Kevin was transferred to Brookdale Greenwood Village Nursing Home.

He was allowed to see Bear for a couple of minutes as they loaded him in the ambulance. I was surprised Bear wasn't excited to see him. Kevin had lost significant weight and probably smelled like the hospital, but Bear was almost afraid to go near him. That was sad, but Bear had been through a lot too.

We followed the ambulance to Brookdale, but they made me leave everything in the lobby when we got there. I have to say; I wasn't crazy about leaving all his personal belongings by the front door.

As difficult as it was to leave him, I praised God for another wonderful day with this great man. The past forty-three days were brutal, but sometimes, you must fall down for God to lift you up.

Kevin was required to be in quarantine for 14 days. It didn't matter if Guy and I were vaccinated; state law says no visitation.

The transfer was harsh, as Kevin and I had only been apart for six days since he moved to Colorado eight years ago. The hardest part was not knowing how Kevin was being treated or if he was having problems. I had been his full-time physical therapist for the past six weeks. I was the one who exercised his arms and legs every day. I read to him and played his music. I fed him his meals and got his ice water, except for an hour or two at lunchtime when Guy came to visit.

❧📖❧

By morning Brookdale had moved Kevin to a new room next to the nurse's station. I don't think they realized how much care he would need. He was completely helpless at this point.

I spent the day working on our bills, setting up post-discharge doctor appointments, getting him a primary care physician, and trying to get Kevin's phone working again.

Our bills got messed up when I couldn't get into Kevin's online banking account. I just sent an estimated payment to every account holding us through December. That gave me time to figure out how to get a paper bill sent to the house.

I called Brookdale and tried to get a schedule of Kevin's therapy and meals so I would know when to call him, but they didn't follow a schedule.

I talked to Kevin, but he didn't recognize my voice or have any idea who I was. He kept talking about leaving Brookdale in a black bag. He thought I had left him there to die, which ripped my heart. I tried to reassure him that he would be okay, and I promised to see him as soon as they lifted the quarantine.

The move was too hard on him. I wished I had waited another day or two before the move. He was backsliding again. He needed someone familiar to attend to him. Isolation is something they do to unruly prisoners, not to sick people. I tried not to freak out and let God handle it, but it was so hard not to be there. Each day was a test of faith.

"Thank you, Lord, for doing exceedingly more than we could imagine. Please give me strength in the coming days. Thirteen more to get through."

I read from the devotional *Jesus Calling* by Sarah Young each morning after my prayers. I received two of these books as gifts from Kevin's family. So many times, it was just the right words of encouragement. I found myself surprisingly calm when I compared my current stress level to that of the first week of Kevin's illness.

My devotional reading that day was, "Hope is the golden cord connecting you to heaven. This cord helps you hold your head high, even when multiple trials are buffeting you. I will never leave your side, and I will never let go of your hand. But without the cord of hope, your head may slump, and your feet may shuffle as you journey uphill with Me. Hope lifts your perspective from your weary feet to the glorious view you can see from the high road. You are reminded that the road we're traveling together is ultimately the highway to heaven. When you consider this radiant destination, the roughness or smoothness of the road ahead becomes much less significant. I am training you to hold a dual focus in your heart: My continual presence and the hope of heaven."

❧📖❧

On Tuesday, I continued to work on paying bills to keep me from worrying about Kevin. I couldn't get into his computer to find our monthly bills, so I called all the companies to ask them to switch me to paper billing. Almost without fail, the companies told me they needed Kevin's permission to make any changes. I sent them a copy of my Power of Attorney weeks ago. Still, only two companies accepted the notarized form. Even the credit card that was in my name, and had been for more than thirty years, refused to change me to paper billing. They claimed they couldn't do anything until they heard from Kevin and his online banking account. They would give me the balance over the phone and take my banking information to pay the balance over the phone, but said they couldn't send me a bill. I sent them a check with the receipt from an old invoice and paid the balance plus a thousand dollars in case there was an automatic charge I didn't remember. I did the same for all the utilities and insurance.

American Express and Sam's Club accepted the Power of Attorney. I had to open an entirely new Xcel Natural Gas account even though this account at this address had been in my name for more than twenty years. Then they wanted me to send them a new customer deposit.

I know electronic bill paying is the wave of the future, but it really sucks when the bill payer is incapacitated. I hate to be a Boomer about new technology, but this has been a nightmare. I advise everyone to have an emergency plan in place.

"Dear Jesus, thank you for the many miracles you have shown me over the last forty-four days. When I start to lose faith, please help me focus on what is important, Your Love and Your Grace. Please heal Kevin's mind and restore his strength. Please watch over the caregivers as they dedicate themselves to healing. Bless his family and friends for the support they have given us. I know that not everyone has their prayers answered so favorably, and my heart aches for those who have lost loved ones or still have family and loved ones in the ICU. In Jesus' name, Amen."

Brookdale took Kevin off quarantine Wednesday morning. The nurse asked me how fast I could get to the rehabilitation center. I said thirty minutes, but I made it in twenty-five. Thank you, Lord, for another answered prayer. She mentioned that the entire facility might go on lockdown for a week but promised to let me know. I prayed that wouldn't happen. I went crazy being away from him for only a single day.

I was so excited to get to Brookdale that I left a pot of chicken stock simmering on the stove. I remembered several hours later. I called Guy, who lives next door. The stock was ruined, but he saved the pan.

Kevin was with the speech therapist when I arrived. She was also his physical therapist. She told us Kevin would be at Brookdale for quite a while. Her estimate was four to five months.

It was so heartwarming to see him out of bed and sitting in a wheelchair. The most he had done at the hospital was briefly sitting on the bedside with help. He was shaking, and nothing he said made sense, but at least he recognized me.

It was painful for him to sit in the chair. His back and neck muscles were so weak he couldn't hold his head up. He asked for a head support, and the nurse said she would get one, but she didn't return.

At about 1:00 pm, the therapist took him to the workout room to practice standing. I found that hard to fathom since he couldn't even sit without help. I waited in his room. While he was gone, I set out his personal belongings.

When he returned from rehab, he was exhausted and talking nonstop nonsense. I helped him eat dinner, rubbed his feet, and adjusted his bed. I changed his diaper and dressed him in new pajamas for the night. When I left at 9:00 pm, I wasn't sure he still knew who I was.

My nightly prayers were once more filled with requests and tears. Looking back on the last forty-five days, I can see where the Holy Spirit carried me. My friends kept telling me how strong I was, and I told them, "It isn't me; it's God's work. I could never have done this alone."

෮📖෧

The following day, Brookdale was on complete lockdown again. They told me there could be no visitors until further notice.

An employee had tested positive for COVID. Although the employee was on self-quarantine, they were required to test all remaining staff and all residents before reopening. They estimated up to a week to get everyone tested.

Even though they wouldn't let me see Kevin, I took Bear to visit, hoping the familiar would keep Kevin grounded. I told our friends and family to call him.

He was locked in a strange place, and I believed familiar voices were crucial to his sanity. I wanted Kevin to know he hadn't been forgotten.

I called him three times, and he was somewhat coherent. I hoped he would settle in. It's incredible how thankful I can feel for little things like having him tell me what he had for breakfast.

Even though I was apart from Kevin, I knew God was with him. Our God is the great healer. I will always be grateful for my time with this sweet man. I praised God for all His miracles, large and small. I thanked the Lord that Kevin and I had the opportunity to travel the country in 2020.

I talked to him several times on Friday. Most of the time, Kevin was clear, but he still had relapses of aphasia. Only once while I was talking to him did he say he would be departing in a black bag. I reassured him I would be there soon to bring him back home. It didn't sound like they would lift the quarantine before Sunday or Monday. I brought Bear to visit every morning in case they lifted it sooner. I didn't understand why I couldn't be with Kevin. We had been together every day since June 14th, apart from the past Tuesday.

On Saturday, Brookdale was still on lockdown and wouldn't even let Bear visit Kevin. I was so distraught. This seclusion was torture. I know he had nurses with him, but that isn't the same as having family or familiar faces. He wasn't sure of his surroundings, and they took away everyone who would be recognizable. It had to be terrifying. I missed him so much.

I called Kevin to tell him about the Fundraiser our friends put together. I've always been uncomfortable being the center of attention. This trial has shown me that I can't do everything alone. I needed help every day, and the Lord sent our friends. I was genuinely humbled by their generosity and love.

Sunday, August 1st, was the cruelest day since June 14th. The calls to Kevin were unbearable. He was talking in circles again, making no sense. He didn't know me and kept saying he would be dead by morning. He claimed the nurses were trying to kill him. He was so afraid and in agony.

I needed to be with him. Certainly, the staff wasn't trying to hurt him, but I knew what kind of care he needed. I cried all day. I felt like I was going to lose my mind. I was helpless to soothe his anguish and pain. I needed to find a way to be with him. I thought about bringing him home, but I knew I couldn't handle his therapy without help from professionals.

I studied the brochure Brookdale gave me, praying for an answer. The answer was there.

You have been given this mountain to show others that the mountain can be moved.

I called Brookdale Monday morning and asked if I could be a companion/sitter and quarantine with Kevin. According to their rules, I was allowed to request a full-time companion if I was willing to pay for it. They had roll-away beds, and I could buy my own meals. Guy was willing to take care of Bear, so I had no reason to stay home. Being his companion would allow me to help Kevin with his meals, combing his hair, brushing his teeth, bathing, and general exercise. Mostly, my being there would reassure him that he hadn't been forgotten and left there to die.

The admissions director said she didn't think that would be possible. An hour later, they called back and gave me special permission to quarantine with Kevin. They wouldn't let me stay overnight, but I was allowed to be there from 8:00 am to 8:00 pm.

Another prayer was answered. Praise God. He was with me every step of the way.

When I got to Kevin's room, he was still talking in circles but far better than he had been on the phone the past three days. He was much less angry. He even joked with the doctor a bit. I think seeing me really helped him relax. The next time there is a major pandemic, I hope they note how important it is to have family involved.

When it was time for me to leave, he made me promise to come back. That tugged at my heart that he might think I wouldn't return in the morning.

≈📖≪

I had hoped the roller coaster was over, but Kevin had a rough day on Wednesday. Primarily his concentration and having trouble remembering what happened the day before. He tried to tell me I hadn't visited and thought he had only been at Brookdale for two days. I tried to tell him he had transferred more than a week ago, but he wasn't having it. He didn't believe he had lost an entire week. In all honesty, he was out of it most of the week.

He felt like he couldn't do his therapy and refused to get out of bed. His therapists pushed him hard to keep him progressing, but Kevin was frustrated, agitated, overwhelmed, and discouraged. It was evident in his voice and words.

Kevin was usually an optimistic person. He joked with the nurses the day they took him off the ventilator. I feared that Kevin wouldn't be the same person after this. Some of the changes were due to all the medication he was taking. He was on twelve different medications, including an antipsychotic.

He kept saying he needed a day off to recover, or he would only break down more muscle. He was a runner and a weightlifter, so he probably knew what he was talking about. I was torn; I believed the therapist should know what was best for him.

When I felt like he was giving up, I would get scared, and then I would get short with him. I wanted him to get better, but all I knew was my own experiences. If I were in his place, I would have given up about the time the strokes happened in June. I have never been one to exercise, even if I'm not in great pain, as Kevin was. Because I'm a lazy person at heart, I feared the worst would overcome Kevin.

"Lord, give me patience. Lord, I know You will do things in Your own time. Lord, please forgive me for my shortness with him. I know he can't help the pain. Please give me the strength and calmness to be the inspiration he needs to get better. Please clear his mind and give him the strength to rebuild his muscles without undue pain. In Jesus' Holy name, Amen."

❧📖❧

By the end of the second week at Brookdale, Kevin could transfer from the bed and back with the help of a strong therapist. I even got to take him outside for a while. It is incredible what sunshine can do for the soul. It is a gift from God that is so often overlooked or taken for granted. Lord, forgive my impatience. Only ten days ago, Kevin couldn't even sit in a chair.

Guy was a saint through all of this. He took care of Bear and helped me with errands. Guy was the caretaker for his mother in her last years. He made her meals and played cards or Scrabble with her every day. Even when she could no longer care for herself, Guy got her up, put her to bed, and changed her clothing. When I think of a good Christian man, Guy comes to mind. He is so selfless.

For the remainder of the week, Kevin had a few rough days, but overall, he improved rapidly. He had an in-room doctor's appointment with the staff doctor who started weaning him off his steroids. Kevin's oxygen was off for forty minutes before the nurse noticed, so they began weaning him off it as well. He seemed more relaxed but demanded that I bring him a big calendar so he could see what day it was.

On the way home, I dropped some cupcakes off to thank the ICU caregivers at the Hospital. One of Kevin's nurses told me the staff had been very impressed with the love and support of Kevin's family and friends. They honestly didn't think he would have survived without the abundance of love he received.

Prayers are a mighty gift, and time is a precious commodity. I sincerely thank everyone for your time and for showing me the way.

I can't tell you how happy I am to have found Jesus Christ. So many times, when I started to struggle, I would say a little prayer and feel the weight lifted. Praise God for his love and grace. I am a witness to the miracles of our creator. The Lord answered our prayers day after day. I want to shout it from the rooftops because I have been blessed beyond reason.

Romans 8:28
And we know that all things work together for good to those who love God, to those who are the called according to His purpose.
(NKJV)

We spent Sunday watching Church by the Glades and reading the bible. Later I mailed out thank you notes to all the people who responded to Kevin's Go Fund Me Page. It still boggles my mind that so many people reached out to help us.

I believe that's what Jesus meant when he talked about his Church. It isn't a building or a religion; it's people who love each other and take care of each other. I am so humbled. Thank you, Jesus, for the love of our friends and family. They are truly remarkable and were my inspirational guide throughout this trial. Thank you, Lord, for every step forward. Thank you, Jesus, for giving me this calling.

Kevin made steady progress throughout the week. By day fifty-five, Kevin no longer needed a speech therapist and was eating a regular diet. He could take a couple of steps and rarely required the Hoyer Lift. Each day his mind was sharper, and his speech was clearer.

It was my need; to see him improve each day. I hung on to every advancement he made.

I told him, "There will be no more backsliding. My heart can't take it."

On Saturday, August 7th, Kevin took a shower for the first time since June 10th. That was fantastic. His hair was gunked-up with hair products that were supposed to clean it. It was hard to transfer from the wheelchair to the shower chair, but it was healthy work. They even let me roll up my pant legs and get in the shower with him. We happily scrubbed off two months of hospital grime. Then we went outside to let his hair dry in the sun. It was a beautiful summer day.

There is a difference between happiness and joy. Happiness is fleeting. Sunshine, puppies, and good food can make you happy, but joy wells up from deep inside. It feels like love for everything and everyone; your heart wants to burst with passion. Even during the tough times, when I outwardly feel fear or frustration, I feel a sense of joy deep in my being. Thank you, Jesus, for this.

≈📖≈

It was now August eighth, and Brookdale was still on lockdown. It seemed like they had to start all over again as soon as they finished testing. I'm so very glad they let me take care of him every day. I don't know what I would have done if they had refused to let me in. I empathize with people in nursing or retirement homes who never got to see their families because of the pandemic.

I came in early to help Kevin get his day started. There was never anyone at the front desk, and the door was open at 5:00 am for staff, so I started arriving at 6:00 each morning.

After dressing, I read our daily devotional to him. Then we watched the Church by the Glades online service. Kevin dosed off most of the day. He worked hard at his physical therapy all week and enjoyed having Sunday off.

He was immersed in the news when I left for the night. He had been watching non-stop news since they fixed his television. He bounced back and forth between CNN and Fox. Both stations make him angry. The rise in terrorism in Afghanistan was scary. I didn't know how the US could pull out without losing thousands of people and military supplies. I kept trying to get Kevin to watch something less dire to no avail.

On Monday, the doctor and therapists said Kevin was doing excellent and wanted to train me to care for him at home. We needed to make a few modifications to the house, but it was doable. The doctor thought Kevin would be at Brookdale for at least three or four more weeks. That had us hoping for the weekend of the Libertarian Party's 50th Anniversary.

Kevin needed to get in and out of bed by himself and walk to the bathroom. Once he was home, he would have to walk to the bathroom and his exercise equipment.

I learned one of the biggest lessons of my life over the months of Kevin's illness. Let go and let God. Every morning I turned my troubles over to Jesus. My problems didn't go away, but they no longer feel insurmountable. When I started to feel angry or overwhelmed, I asked Jesus to help me. He has never let me down. He gives me a sense of peace I have never known before. Every day is a gift. Thank you, Lord Jesus.

The quarantine was lifted on Tuesday, so Guy covered for me at lunchtime. The break allowed me to run some much-needed errands. I went to the bank and finally got Kevin's phone unlocked. Having his phone made Kevin happy, and that made me happy.

He was still arguing about how long he had been at Brookdale and what days I did or did not visit. Now he added the times he had or had not done therapy. Since I took his vitals three times a day and recorded them in a notebook, I added everything we did during the day. It was kind of a journal. This was an experience I would not forget.

The nurse practitioner stopped by and said she was pleased with Kevin's progress but told us it might be a couple of months before he could go home. That was depressing. I felt like a Yo-Yo; whenever I thought Kevin was ready to go home, he would relapse, or someone would tell me it would take much longer.

I asked the nurse for something for his runny nose. She said the doctor would order something. I wasn't allowed to bring anything in.

He spent most of the day watching the news channels. I tried to get him to shut the television off before I left for the night, but he wasn't having it. I must have napped too long in the afternoon.

I couldn't do this without looking to Jesus every day. I sincerely hope others, who have been given similar roads to travel, can find peace through God. It really was an amazing experience. I thank the Lord for his incredible gifts. I am forever changed.

≈📖≈

August twelfth was memorable because Kevin's nephew, Little Guy, reached out to wish him well. The children in Little Guy's church prayed for Kevin's healing. We listened to the audio file. It was so precious that we both cried. These are the moments I will take with me to the grave. These are the moments that show me God is real.

After his weekly shower, they weighed Kevin at 163 pounds. He was over 200 before he got sick. Sadly, it was all muscle loss.

Kevin wanted to eat dinner in bed instead of in his chair. I know he was tired, and he was getting restless. He had been at Brookdale for just over two weeks. He wanted to go home, but I couldn't handle his care alone. I tried to explain this to him, but I don't think he believed me.

I took Kevin's laundry home that night. It is part of the Brookdale service, but it was easier than counting on the staff to keep his things straight. Since he was wearing regular clothing, I was happy to do this. It made me feel useful. So many things were out of my control that laundry became a blessing.

I'm thankful I didn't have to squeeze in a job and children through all this. If I had to choose a time for Kevin to spend three months in the hospital, I don't think I could have come up with a better choice. We were both retired. We had traveled the country last year, and then we lost our bid for seats on the Libertarian Party of Colorado State Board. Hence, we really had nothing better to do. God's timing is impeccable.

"Do not be afraid" is written in the bible 365 times. That's a daily reminder from God to live fearless every day.

By day eighteen at Brookdale Rehabilitation Center, Kevin could sit in an armchair and eat his meals without help. He needed a towel for a bib, but it could have been, and had been, so much worse. I clearly remember the discussions of ventilators and gastral feeding tubes.

Kevin loves food and cooking. At one time, the hospital counselor told me Kevin would never be able to cook again. I never gave up hope.

He could get in and out of bed with my help for the first time. We had seen the last of the Hoyer lift.

The nurse started Kevin on an antihistamine for a runny nose he had the past few days. I wasn't sure if it was a cold, allergies, or the cannula. It was frustrating to wait nearly a week for a change in medication, especially when it was something like a cold tablet.

I showed Kevin all the people who donated to his Go Fund Me Page. The contributions more than covered the cost of the new sidewalk we needed to prepare the house for Kevin's return. This brought tears to Kevin's eyes.

Kerry, Jack, and Erowyn arrived that morning. They were moving from New Hampshire back to Lopez Island in Washington. When I got home, they had made salmon with roasted potatoes for dinner. Oh, how I had missed having Kerry cook for me at night. Kerry planned to stay a couple of months to help me with Kevin's rehabilitation.

∻ 📖 ∽

Starting on Sunday of the third week at Brookdale, Kevin had a setback with his oxygen. He dropped to 66% overnight and had to go back on the cannula at 6:00 am. I had hoped his lungs were healed enough to stop the steroids and the cannula, but it looked like he would have to stay on oxygen longer. He was thoroughly disheartened.

He still struggled with confusion. It was impossible to know if the dementia was from steroids or other medication. Only time would tell us if he would ever regain his mental acuity.

We watched the service from Church by the Glades after breakfast. The sermon was about surrendering everything to God. Some people dip their toes in the water or maybe get in knee-deep. God wants us to swim in his love and trust him to care for us.

"Thank you, Lord Jesus, for the many blessings you have given me. I'm surely in over my head, but I know You will save me."

I arrived at 6:00 am on Monday to wake Kevin and help him prepare for the day. His oxygen was in the seventies when I checked his vitals. The nurse had him do some deep breathing and said he was fine. I asked to see the doctor because he shouldn't drop below 90%.

About an hour later, a lab technician came to X-ray his chest.

The doctor saw Kevin at about 10:00 and said the X-ray and labs looked good. I wasn't convinced. I had spent the past sixty days monitoring Kevin's blood pressure, heart rate, and oxygen. I felt certain something wasn't right. He had been entirely off oxygen support for the past eleven days and had no trouble staying in the nineties. He now required three liters of oxygen and struggled to stay in the low nineties.

I tried to concentrate on puzzles while Kevin watched the refugees fleeing Afghanistan. The news was bleak. It's hard to know what this might mean for the United States. I didn't know what to do to help, so I just prayed for them.

At the end of the day, Kevin's blood pressure was high, and the nurse told him to shut off the news. I went home hoping the next day would be better and said my prayers of thanks for another beautiful day with Kevin.

It was hard to believe my life had changed so much in less than a year. I was thankful for having had the opportunity to travel. I would never have imagined I could spend that much time in a nineteen-foot trailer and not go crazy.

We had some bumps along the way. In early November, while watching the sunset on the Outer Banks of North Carolina, we lost the keys to the truck. We were ten miles from our camper. Everything was closed because it was off-season. There were no taxis or hotel rooms, so we slept in the truck the first night. We called a friend and asked her to mail us our spare keys. The next night, we got a cabin at the KOA, but there were no linens or blankets. We used the towels in the back of the truck for a blanket. I could have gotten upset or angry since it was quite cold, but I chalked it up to an interesting experience.

On Tuesday, August eighteenth, I faced an entirely different type of experience. At this point, a good day was any day I could spend with Kevin and see him improve. On the bad days, the bumps are genuinely terrifying.

When I arrived at Brookdale, Kevin's oxygen was at 71%, and he had a terrible headache. I was distraught. At the hospital, the alarms went off anytime Kevin's oxygen dropped below 85%. When he stayed low for more than a few minutes, the nurses increased the oxygen on his machine.

Even with concentrated breathing, Kevin could barely get his blood oxygen back into the nineties. The nurse raised the oxygen concentrator to five liters, the highest he could go on a regular canula. If he needed more, he would need to return to Adventist and the high-flow breathing machines.

All my emotional alarms went crazy. I told the nurse to call the doctor. I said, "He needs to go to the hospital. He's getting worse, not better."

He spent the day in bed watching television while I waited to hear from the doctor. Although the backslide was disappointing, I reminded myself that I had sixty-five days with Kevin because of God's grace. Kevin beat the odds several times.

I hated leaving that night because Kevin was still laboring to breathe, and the doctor never came by. I was probably being a Helicopter mom, but I couldn't help worrying. I knew I should have let go and let God take care of it, but that was a whole lot harder to do than to say.

❧📖❧

Have you ever had a moment when everything around you came crashing down? August nineteenth was like that. Tomorrow is never guaranteed, so make the most of today.

Only four days earlier, Kevin was standing with his walker and taking steps. Only four days earlier, we believed he would be attending the 50th Anniversary Party. Only four days earlier, we thought he would be coming home in a week.

I arrived at Brookdale Wednesday morning, and Kevin's oxygen was at 54% on five liters of O2. I felt like I was going to lose my mind with worry and anger. I told the nurses on both Monday and Tuesday that something was wrong. Each time, they would make Kevin try to breathe deeper. When he would get into the upper eighties, they would say, "He's okay."

No, he was not okay! He should have been able to get into the upper nineties with deep breaths. I checked my own oxygen to make sure the Oxygen reader was working. I was ninety-seven to ninety-nine every time.

I went to the nurse's station and demanded to see a doctor. When the doctor arrived, she looked at me and said, "He needs to go to the hospital."

All I could think was, I've been telling the nurses this for two days. I didn't say it. I just nodded and said, "Please." I was so thankful they were listening.

An ambulance came to take Kevin to the hospital. The EMTs wanted to take him to Sky Ridge because it was closer, but we demanded they take him back to Adventist Hospital in Parker. The staff there knew Kevin and his extensive history. After about fifteen minutes, they agreed to take him to Adventist.

I tried to be understanding through all the drama. I can honestly say I was a saint compared to how I would have reacted only a year ago. I was not yet where I wanted to be, but I was far from where I had been.

Colossians 1:11
Being strengthened with all power according to his glorious might so that you may have great endurance and patience.
(NIV)

After three hours in the emergency room, Kevin was transferred back to the ICU to his previous room. I was surprised but glad they allowed me to stay with him this time.

His doctor said, "I'll say this as politely as I can; your lungs are full of crap and look horrible." Then he added, "You still look better than the first time I saw you."

I prayed every time I felt overwhelmed. The anger and fear would slip out every now and then, and I'd say things I regretted. Without this new-found faith, I know this tribulation would have been beyond my ability to bear. I prayed for peace, a calm mind, and no more tears.

Mark 9

*24 Immediately the father of the child cried out and said
with tears, "Lord, I believe, help my unbelief."*
(NKJV)

Kevin handled the setback far better than me. He was friendly and joking with the staff. After I left for the night, he was moved to a regular room. It was an actual standard room, like for just ordinary sick people on the first floor.

God's work and drugs are amazing. It had been a scary week, but Kevin was feeling a thousand times better by Saturday.

There are times when God speaks to us so clearly. Our Saturday devotion was particularly fitting. We read it several times.

The daily devotion was about healing. It was about asking for healing and being thankful for what restoration God has granted. God heals on His own time, and hardships bring us closer to God because it is then, in our difficulties, that we are reminded how much we need Him.

With this in mind, I thanked God for my blessed life. I could have been born blind or missing a limb. I could have been born poor in the Middle East or India. I could have been born to parents who were drug addicts or worse. God blessed me with a loving family in a beautiful country with good health. Most of all, when I was lost, He gave me Kevin. It was through this relationship that I was led back to Jesus. I praise the Lord. The joy outweighs the sorrow a hundred-fold.

Kevin transferred back to Brookdale around 5:00 pm on Saturday. I had barely organized all his things in his hospital room before it was time to pack it up again, but I was so happy to do it.

Kevin said it felt almost like coming home when we returned to Brookdale. All the attendants were glad to see us. So often, when a patient leaves a nursing home in an ambulance, they don't return.

Yes, you will rise from the ashes, but the burning comes first. For this, you must be brave. -Kalen Dion-

❧📖❧

After the past week's drama, Sunday was one of those perfect days we rarely get. God is truly good. It was hard to believe Kevin had been in the hospital for seventy days.

He used the toilet for the first time since June 14th. It was one of the hurdles he needed to overcome before returning home. By this time, he could feed himself and brush his teeth. It may sound like nothing, but only two weeks ago, he couldn't sit in a chair or lift his head off the pillow.

I ordered a steak from Out Back Steak House for his dinner to celebrate his short turnaround at Adventist. Afterward, we watched gospel shows until it was time for me to go home.

He was susceptible to setbacks for the remainder of his rehabilitation. Still, we trusted Jesus to bring him home sooner rather than later.

If you had known me before this trial, you would shake your head. I never liked gospel music, watching religious services, daily devotions, or nightly prayers. Through the remainder of August, I couldn't get enough of God. I listened to Grace FM Bible studies daily on my way to and from Brookdale. I listened to Bill Pierce every night before I went to sleep.

The hospital choice had a lot to do with my conversion. Their love and care made a huge difference in my outlook. People who dedicate their lives to others in the name of God are truly extraordinary.

Every day I would listen to Gospel music, and many songs touched me deeply. My favorite song was:

> Thank you, for giving to the Lord,
> I am a life that was changed.
> Thank you, for giving to the Lord
> I am so glad you gave.

As I listened, I dedicated the song to those who donated the artwork to Adventist Hospital, the tireless nurses and doctors, the pastors who prayed with us each day, and those who prayed for us over the months.

❧ 📖 ❦

During the final week of August, Kevin's mobility improved vastly, bordering on the miraculous. Even the staff workers were amazed by the speed of his healing. In preparation for Kevin to return home, I hired someone to tear out the old stone walkway and put in something wheelchair friendly. I had my father's shower chair, wheelchair, and Hover-Round, along with a few other medical items we needed for Kevin's rehabilitation.

The maintenance man from Brookdale brought in a recliner, so Kevin no longer had to sit in straight-back armchairs or bed. I was glad because now he didn't have to stay in bed all day.

By this time, he started doing his own Facebook posts. He still struggled with the keyboard due to his shaking, but it was so good to see him interacting with other people. It didn't hurt that Facebook got him away from the television news programs.

I celebrated when Kevin took the first step, even though it was all he could do. By the end of August, he could get out of bed and walk to the bathroom with his walker. In fact, he could walk the entire length of the hall, nearly forty feet. He still had a long road ahead, but we trusted Jesus to lead us in the direction God intended for us, whatever that might be.

Of course, there were still things that could set him back weeks or even months, but we prayed daily that these would be the last days at Brookdale.

While Guy spent the afternoons with Kevin, I arranged the house for his return. The music room became our bedroom, and the dining room became a home gym. I moved the recliner from the library upstairs to the music room so he could watch television, knowing he wouldn't be able to use the living room television until he could negotiate the stairs. I installed handicap bars for the tub and toilet.

God answered so many of my prayers, even those for friends who were suffering. This was truly amazing to me. When Kevin or I were having a frustrating day, we would stop and say a little prayer, and the fear, anger, and anxiety would melt away.

Those who have had a relationship with Jesus understand what I'm saying and are not the least surprised. My friends who have not experienced this may scoff and think it's a coincidence or wishful thinking. I used to believe that. No matter what happens from here, I am a changed person.

The next day I brought Kevin new shoes. I don't know what happened to the ones he wore when he arrived at the hospital last June or the shirt and pants he was wearing. All I got back was his watch. And him, I got him back, and that's all I cared about.

We took a regular Uber to Adventist hospital for a CT scan. He still needed the wheelchair to get around but didn't complain about the pain. He said it still hurt, but it was tolerable. Then he had a doctor's appointment with Gastral Internist. The internist was amazed at how far Kevin had come. He gave Kevin a clean bill of health, and we talked about politics for a while. Apparently, the doctor is a Libertarian, too. The visits were good, but they wore him out.

The therapist had Kevin practice transferring from his wheelchair to a car. The Toyota sat low to the ground, but Kevin got in and out twice. Once more, I was in awe of God's power to heal and his mercy on us.

1 John 5
14 Now this is the confidence that we have in Him, that if we ask anything according to His will, He hears us. 15 And if we know that He hears us, whatever we ask, we

know that we have the petitions that we have asked of Him.
(NKJV)

Kevin was discharged into my care on Friday morning, September first, eighty days after his cardiac arrest. I praised God daily that Kevin recovered far beyond all expectations.

❧📖❧

An incredible peace can be found when you let God take over. People often asked how I was holding up, and I would say, "Jesus is taking care of me; I'm fine." And I was fine. Because He was with me, I could spend fourteen hours a day in the ICU. All the responsibilities of this world faded and became unimportant. I didn't want to waste one moment of the gift of time with Kevin God had given me.

So often during those first three months, I prayed for strength and guidance. I tried to read Kevin's Bible, but The Kings English is like trying to read Shakespeare. With the guidance of Kevin's fantastic family, I learned how to speak with God.

Job 32:8
But it is the spirit in a person, the breath of the
Almighty, that gives them understanding.
(NIV)

Every night and every morning, I got on my knees and thanked God for His gift, feeling guilty and not understanding why I was spared when so many others had lost loved ones.

God gives us all trials, some beyond imagining; when a child dies before the age of five; when a newlywed wife dies suddenly; when a veteran has PTSD so damaging he can't hold a job; the list is endless. When we are hurting, lost, or afraid, we reach out to God. In our hour of need, He is trying to connect with us and teach us something. Open your heart and try to understand the message. Try to set aside the anger and pain. Trust in Him. We really have no control. Let go and Let God.

"Thank you, Lord Jesus. You have blessed me in ways I cannot put into words. I felt comforted and carried by God's love. He dried my tears during my weakest moments. He gave me peace when I had no control. Thank you, Lord Jesus, Amen."

∽📖∾

God knows what he wants from us in this life. In November, Kevin and I looked at several properties at lower elevations. We were hoping to move back to South Dakota near family, both his and mine. I dreamed of opening a fellowship hall and coffee shop in Valley Springs. Since we would be close to my mom, we could support her church and bring in new blood.

The rush to move to lower ground changed in December because Kevin's oxygen requirements dropped to only needing two liters of oxygen at night. When the third property fell through, it was a clear sign that we were meant to stay in Colorado. I realized I was trying to force God's will.

We started attending Calvary Church Cherry Creek (C-4) on January 2nd. The members of this church were so warm and welcoming. It was the same feeling as Applewood Baptist Church, where I was baptized at twelve. It's not a large church, but it felt like home.

It's been just over a year, and every Sunday, after church at C-4, we watch the online service from Church by the Glades. The music is modern and not my style, but the message is always great. That's saying something since, until the autumn of 2021, sermons always put me to sleep. I encourage all my friends to check out these wonderful churches. Even if, no, especially if you don't regularly attend church.

We listen to bible study classes on the radio. Kevin used to teach bible study, and I love learning more about the bible. When C-4 offered a course on the Torah, we joined the study group, and shortly after, we added the Wednesday night service.

I still check Kevin's weight, blood pressure, temperature, oxygen, and heart rate daily. He takes about ten different pills a day and probably will for the rest of his life. We also check his blood every Monday morning to monitor the blood thinners.

The process of rebuilding muscles is slow and sometimes frustrating, but each day is just a little better. I'm so proud of him for working so hard. He does core and leg workouts three times a week and arms and upper body three days a week. We rest on Sunday.

Kevin is enthusiastic about doing his daily exercises. I'm terrible. Had I been in his place, I would have given up months ago. It helps that Kevin has run five marathons. You don't do that without dedication to daily training.

During his last appointment, the pulmonologist said Kevin was doing fantastic, considering all he went through. In the hospital, the doctor said the scar tissue in his lungs would never heal, but his last pulmonary test was normal and clear. An overnight sleep test showed he stops breathing seventy times an hour, so he now uses a computerized ASV machine for sleep apnea. He no longer needs the oxygen concentrator or cannula; his latest MRI showed only old lesions and no new events.

While Kevin will never be as strong as he once was, he is far stronger than I had dared to hope. He can do everything he used to do except run. We are still working on that.

Jeremiah 18
¹The word which came to Jeremiah from the LORD, saying: ²"Arise and go down to the potter's house, and there I will cause you to hear My words." ³Then I went down to the potter's house, and there he was, making something at the wheel. ⁴And the vessel that he made of clay was marred in the hand of the potter; so he made it again into another vessel, as it seemed good to the potter to make. ⁵Then the word of the LORD came to me, saying: ⁶"O house of Israel, can I not do with you as this potter?" says the LORD. "Look, as the clay is in the potter's hand, so are you in My hand, O house of Israel!
(NKJV)

2 Corinthians 12
⁹And He said to me, "My grace is sufficient for you, for My strength is made perfect in weakness." Therefore most gladly I will rather boast in my infirmities, that the power of Christ may rest upon me.
(NKJV)

Closing

Philippians 1
[9] And this is my prayer: that your love may abound more and more in knowledge and depth of insight, [10] so that you may be able to discern what is best and may be pure and blameless for the day of Christ, [11] filled with the fruit of righteousness that comes through Jesus Christ—to the glory and praise of God.
(NIV)

This was a life-altering experience for both of us. While I often wished the road had not been so challenging, I understand this is the journey God designed. The place I am now could not have been reached by another path. I am full of joy I had not previously known. Yes, I'm tired and sometimes cranky, but I am also at peace.

Ephesians 4
31 *Let all bitterness, wrath, anger clamor, and evil speaking be put away from you, with all malice.* 32 *And be kind to one another, tenderhearted, forgiving one another, even as God in Christ forgave you.*
(NKJV)

Forgiveness is a cornerstone of Christianity. It isn't always easy to forgive, but it is essential. While I forgave many people who hurt me in the past, Caryn and Wayne weighed heavily on my mind.

I wrote a letter to them asking them to forgive me for the negative campaign I ran in 2020. I forgave them for the nasty things they said about me. This is hard because Caryn continues to bully and berate Libertarian friends through her Facebook and podcasts.

They came to our house for a county event in December, and it was difficult to be civil. I am far from being a good Christian, but I know how important it is to keep growing. I must forgive others because God has forgiven me, and what a wretched creature I am to be forgiven.

For now, I skip over anything written by Caryn or about Caryn. Until I'm stronger in my faith, I won't tempt myself. I'll stay away from Libertarian gossip.

I have always liked the following song, but now it has a new meaning.

> Amazing Grace,
> How sweet the sound,
> That saved a wretch like me.
> I once was lost but now am found,
> Was blind but now I see.

Our morning devotions have been a great way to start each day. After all, we have been through, I don't think I'll ever forget to be thankful, but it doesn't hurt to be reminded.

This has been an amazing journey. I sincerely thank everyone for their prayers, and I thank the Lord for answering those prayers.

Kevin and I didn't do anything – this was, and is, all God's work. Grace is being given something you haven't earned, while Mercy is not being given the punishment you do deserve.

Although I never want to go through this kind of experience again, I do miss the intensity of God's daily presence in my hour of need. From here until he calls me home, I am His.

Micah 6
*⁸ He has shown you, O mortal, what is good. And what
does the L*ORD *require of you? To act justly and to love
mercy and to walk humbly with your God.*
[NIV]

≈📖≪

Christ came out of heaven to get into us. He
did not die simply so that we might be saved
from a bad conscience or to remove the stain of
past sins. He came to make room in your soul that
his will might be done through you. His Spirit
overcomes us and changes our character.

Christianity is a life that allows Christ to live
in you and do His work through you. Salvation is
more than a change of destination from hell to
heaven after we die; it is to be in Christ here on
earth. *"thy will be done on earth as it is in heaven."*

I can testify to the fact that God changed
me. I now love Gospel music, something I hated
before. I am voracious to learn more about God
and His word. I have read the entire Bible twice,
and I'm working my way through it again in a
different translation. I pray daily, enjoy my
morning devotions, and can't wait for the next
bible study to begin. I never tire of the sermons.

Our church promoted one of the more
remarkable changes in me in early 2023. Although
Kevin and I had been living together since 2013,

we had never married. As Libertarians, we both feel marriage is a religious union, and a state-sanctioned marriage certificate is pointless. A marriage license doesn't create a marriage any more than a driver's license creates a driver.

To protect each other in case of death or illness, we filed all the critical paperwork, like Wills, Power of Attorney, and Property Deeds.

When Kevin and I signed up for a Marriage Retreat, we were told we must be legally married before attending the retreat or serving in the church. I was disheartened because I desperately wanted to give back to God, and the church, for all the blessings God had given me over the previous eighteen months. Serving in the church was a way I could share the love and prayers I was given with others.

Kevin is a part of my soul. I genuinely believe I married him before God on Kevin's deathbed. That was the day I started calling him my husband.

While I connected with Kevin in ways I never connected with either Jeff or Monte, the pastors asked that we complete the paperwork.

Rather than hold firm to my Libertarian principles, we chose to get a marriage license. My church family's feelings are more important to us than making any statement about government overreach.

Yes, I am born again as a new person. Thank you, Lord Jesus Christ.

Corinthians 5:15
He died for everyone so that those who receive his new life
will no longer live for themselves. Instead, they will live for
Christ, who died and was raised for them.
(NLT)

Defining Father

Hebrews 12
[9] Moreover, we have all had human fathers who disciplined us and we respected them for it. How much more should we submit to the Father of spirits and live! [10] They disciplined us for a little while as they thought best; but God disciplines us for our good, in order that we may share in his holiness. [11] No discipline seems pleasant at the time, but painful. Later on, however, it produces a harvest of righteousness and peace for those who have been trained by it.
(NIV)

I want to talk about fathers briefly. Based on my childhood, you might understand why I was never comfortable seeing God as my father. "Our Father who art in heaven," "The Father, the Son, and the Holy Spirit," or "Our Heavenly Father."

Growing up, I didn't have a good relationship with my biological father, and my stepfather was rarely home. As a toddler, I was terrified of making my father angry. I only remember being physically spanked once. I must have been in first or second grade. My little sister and I went to the shopping center about a mile from home and didn't get home until long after dark. My father was livid. Mostly out of fear that something had happened to us, I'm sure. I can remember feeling terrible about scaring him. He gave us a couple of good swats on the butt. He had a temper, and though he never lost it with me, I knew better than to cross him.

At about this same time, my mom made a cake one evening, and someone ate the frosting during the night. He asked each of us, "who ate the frosting off the cake," but no one would admit to it. My father then took each of us into the bedroom, one at a time, starting with the oldest. We were all lined up outside the closed door, listening as we heard the belt hitting and Bette crying. He opened the door and asked again, "who ate the frosting off the cake." No one admitted to it, so it was Robert's turn. Again, he asked who the culprit was but got no response. Belinda went into the bedroom, and we could hear her crying and the belt hitting. I was terrified, but I didn't know who had done the deed. When my father came out and asked again, my little sister admitted to eating the frosting. I was so grateful. Once he had the offender, we all thought she would get a whipping, but instead, he just told her never to do that again.

When the drama was over, Belinda told me that our father was hitting the bed and telling her to cry. He had known who had eaten the frosting, but he wanted my sister to admit it.

❧📖❧

Throughout my life, I didn't know what a father was supposed to be. I didn't have a father who took the time to teach me things that I never quite seemed to grasp. My father got angry when I messed up, but I didn't feel like he still loved me through it all. I didn't believe my father put my needs in front of his own.

I was afraid of my father, but not the kind of fear they mention in the Bible. It wasn't out of fear of hurting, disrespecting, or disappointing him. It was out of fear that he would hurt me; it was fear that he would let me starve or leave me.

I didn't trust him.

֍ 📖 ֍

While writing this book, I researched what it means to be a father. I believe these to be the traits of my biological father:

Provider
He worked hard and always had more than one job, but my father spent most of his money on his toys and hobbies.

Protector
Because he worked and played hard, my father left the child-rearing to my mother. I knew incest and was afraid of my father.

Disciplinarian
My father had a bad temper. While I was rarely the target of his anger, his punishments were often unsuitable and could be quite violent.

Dependability
My father's hobbies took precedence over family. We had babysitters putting us to bed at night when he should have been home with his children.

Involvement

I don't remember any time my father attended any school or church function. I don't believe he ever recognized my needs, talents, or desires.

Compassion
My memory of my father's compassion is limited to when he told us he drowned five puppies in the backyard. It was horrifying, and I never understood how he could do that.

Empathy
He may have had empathy for his friends. It wasn't unusual for him to help a friend move or fix a car. He often put their needs above his family.

Expressive
I was fifty years old before my father said, I love you the first time. Birthday cards and gifts always came from my stepmother.

Valuing of mother
My father criticized my mother constantly. While I never heard him say anything demeaning in front of guests, I overheard many fights. When he was in his seventies, he told me he always loved her and thought she had been a good mother. I was stunned because it seemed out of character for him. I don't believe he ever told my mother he was proud of her.

Contrast the previous with what I now know of our Heavenly Father.

Provider

Genesis 1
29 Then God said, "I give you every seed-bearing plant on the face of the whole earth and every tree that has fruit with seed in it. They will be yours for food. And to all the beasts of the earth and all the birds in the sky and all the creatures that move along the ground—everything that has the breath of life in it—I give every green plant for food." And it was so.
(NIV)

God made the heavens and the earth and every form of food. He provided Manna and drew water from stones in the wilderness for his people. Throughout the Bible, God provided a way when all was lost.

Protector

Hebrews 28
29 By faith the people passed through the Red Sea as on dry land; but when the Egyptians tried to do so, they were drowned.
(NIV)

There are many times God has come to our rescue. When the devil comes knocking, all you need to do is ask for help. He will carry you if you aren't strong enough.

Disciplinarian

Ezekiel 23
⁴⁹ You will suffer the penalty for your lewdness and bear the consequences of your sins of idolatry. Then you will know that I am the Sovereign LORD."
(NIV)

Throughout the Bible, God tried to tell his people to be good. When they refused, he punished them. If your child runs out in the street, you scold them because you want them to be safe. If they do it again, you might have to increase the penalty. This is justice, not cruelty.

Dependability

Hebrews 13
⁸ Jesus Christ is the same yesterday and today and forever.
(NIV)

Hebrews 13
¹⁷ Because God wanted to make the unchanging nature of his purpose very clear to the heirs of what was promised, he confirmed it with an oath.
(NIV)

God has never changed throughout all of history. He is always faithful to his promises.

Involvement:

John 1
17 The Word (the Christ) became flesh (a man) and made his dwelling among us. We have seen his glory, the glory of the one and only Son, who came from the Father, full of grace and truth.
(NIV)

God, in the form of Jesus, walked the earth in human form, experiencing all our earthly emotions, knowing our every thought. He knew hunger, pain, and betrayal. After willingly dying for us, He left us with the Holy Spirit, which is still a part of him, to help us each day.

Compassion

Psalm 78
38 For their heart was not steadfast with Him, nor were they faithful in His covenant. 38 But He, being full of compassion, forgave their iniquity, and did not destroy them. Yes, many a time He turned His anger away, and did not stir up all His wrath; 39 For He remembered that they were but flesh, a breath that passes away and does not come again.
(NKJV)

For all the times we fail Him, God forgives us if only we will repent and ask for His forgiveness. He knows we are weak, but He loves us still.

Empathy

Luke 4
⁵ Then the devil, taking Him up on a high mountain, showed Him all the kingdoms of the world in a moment of time. ⁶ And the devil said to Him, "All this authority I will give You, and their glory; for this has been delivered to me, and I give it to whomever I wish. ⁷ Therefore, if You will worship before me, all will be Yours." ⁸ And Jesus answered and said to him, "Get behind Me, Satan! For it is written, 'You shall worship the LORD your God, and Him only you shall serve.'"
[NKJV]

Jesus lived as one of us so he could know first-hand what it is like to be human. He faced the devil repeatedly and went willingly to the cross to die for us. He came to earth in human form to give us Mercy so that, flawed as we are, we could enter eternity with him.

Expressive

Hebrews 4
¹² For the word of God is alive and active. Sharper than any double-edged sword, it penetrates even to dividing soul

and spirit, joints and marrow; it judges the thoughts and
attitudes of the heart. (NIV)

Every time I read the Bible, I gain a new
perspective on who God is and how much He
loves us.

Valuing of mother

John 2
*¹On the third day there was a wedding in Cana of
Galilee, and the mother of Jesus was there. ²Now both
Jesus and His disciples were invited to the wedding. ³And
when they ran out of wine, the mother of Jesus said to
Him, "They have no wine."*
(NKJV)

For the sake of his mother, Jesus turned water
into wine even though his hour had not yet come.

I tell you this because I wanted you to know that I still loved my earthly father. At times, I was afraid of his anger. I was hurt and infuriated by him, and I didn't always understand him.

I had never dated a man with children until I met Kevin. I can see how much he loves his children and wants to keep them safe, but they are adults now, and he must let them make their mistakes. Still, it breaks his heart to see them hurting.

When the Bible talks about fearing the Lord, I believe it is much like this. God wants you to revere him and respect His power. He also wants you to trust Him to keep you safe.

I believe the Old Testament shows our Heavenly Father trying to teach his young children to be good, loving, and holy. He gave them land and food. He took them out of slavery. For all that, they turned from Him and tried doing things themselves or asking other gods for help.

Mankind was disciplined many times because they just never learned. The New Testament is much like a father caring for his grown children. He has given them all the tools they need to have a wonderful and everlasting life, and it crushes his soul when his children don't take advantage of his amazing gift.

Please, take advantage. It is never too soon.

Author Michele Poague is a member of Calvary Chapel Cherry Creek in Centennial, Colorado (C4). She is the author of the multiple-award-winning trilogy: *The Healing Crystal.* Book 1, *Heir to Power;*  Book 2, *Fall of Eden;* Book 3, *Ransom;* and these standalone novels: *The Candy Store; The Broken Shade; Riding Shotgun;* and *Star of Genesis.* For more information regarding Michele Poague or her published works, please visit michelepoague.com.

Bible translations used:
CSB – Christian Standard Bible
ESV – English Standard Version
KJV – King James Version
NCV – New Century Version
NIV – New International Version
NKJV – New King James Version
NLT – New Living Testament

Songs
Hold On, by Kansas
Amazing Grace, by John Newton
Thank You for Giving to the Lord, by Ray Boltz

Ingram Content Group UK Ltd.
Milton Keynes UK
UKHW010859130723
425071UK00004B/129